"We often wonder why God has us in the places and roles we're in, perhaps because we believe if we were somewhere else doing something else, we could finally be used by the Lord. In *Love Where You Live*, Shauna reminds us that whether God calls us to stay or go, we are a sent people, and therefore our places and roles have divine purpose. Through biblical stories and her own story, she illustrates practical ways we can live as the sent people we are. For those who are new to an area, for those needing fresh eyes for where they already are, and for those needing a jumpstart toward loving their neighbor—you will find this resource immensely helpful."

Christine Hoover, author of several books, including *The Church Planting Wife* and *Searching for Spring: How God Makes All Things Beautiful in Time*

"Many of us say that we want to change the world, but we are not willing to change the way we live out our days in our own neighborhoods. Instead we want to choose the time, place, and level of commitment so that we can compartmentalize it from our nice, neat, clean, daily existence. We have turned the love of the gospel into something we schedule to do rather than something we are. The truth of the matter is if we want to change the world we have to change the way we live and get some daily dirt under our nails in the process. *Love Where You Live* is our practical guide in helping us navigate our neighborhoods, inviting people into our lives, and sharing Jesus."

Todd Adkins, director of LifeWay Leadership at LifeWay Christian Resources

"To really impact this continent with the gospel, we must mobilize every Christian family to engage their neighbors, friends, schoolmates, and coworkers with the good news of Jesus. In *Love Where You Live*, Shauna Pilgreen shares her family's story of moving to San Francisco and becoming salt and light in their community. I pray God will use this book to help tens of thousands of families become the hands and feet of Jesus in their communities."

Kevin Ezell, president of North American Mission Board, SBC

"Shauna Pilgreen has written a holy instruction manual for those who desire to follow God's calling into parts unknown—and she does so with grace, humor, and love. She reminds us that each part of our 'average story' can be used by God to impact those around us."

Lauren K. Denton, *USA Today* bestselling author
of *The Hideaway* and *Hurricane Season*

"If I'm honest, the place I call 'home' has always been about me . . . where I feel comfortable, where I relax, where I retreat. Shauna Pilgreen shattered that perspective and replaced it with a sense of purpose and mission for loving where I live by living sent. This book will challenge you to find meaning and purpose where God has you. Whether you've lived on the same street your entire life or moved every year, *Love Where You Live* will help you see the purpose in the place you call home."

Jenni Catron, author, speaker, and founder of The 4Sight Group

"In *Love Where You Live,* Shauna Pilgreen gives practical insights and strategies for navigating the perils as well as seizing the opportunities to bear fruit where God has planted each of us. A must-read for all of us who are tempted at times to believe that a moving truck is the only acceptable answer to our prayers."

Steve Stroope, lead pastor of Lake Pointe Church
and author of *Tribal Church*

"As Christians one of our chief words is *go*. Abraham had to move, Moses was a vagabond, Jesus called the disciples to leave their nets, and the Great Commission is intended to send us out. Yet we yearn for a mortgage in a quiet neighborhood with good schools, pleading with God 'No, not Africa.' Instead of fear, let's walk in faith. Trusting God's leadership to uproot and replant or just plant us deeper and differently where we live. Shauna has practical principles to help us become difference makers wherever God has planted us. Let her lead you on His journey of joy for you."

Gregg Matte, pastor of Houston's First Baptist Church and
author of *Finding God's Will*

"I know this woman. I love this woman. I trust this woman. That's why I am giving a big shout-out about her book *Love Where You Live*. You must read it! Shauna shows us how to love like Jesus loved, right in our own little corners of the world. Her own messy-beautiful story of learning to 'live sent' right where she's planted is as practical as it is powerful. You'll want to slip on your shoes, walk out your front door, and start loving where you live today."

Jennifer Rothschild, author of *Lessons I learned in the Dark* and *Me, Myself and Lies*

"The message of *Love Where You Live* is essential not just for pastors and Christian leaders but for every follower of Jesus. I've watched Shauna and Ben live out this message in one of the most unreached areas of North America. If the church could get this, it would change everything! This is a must-read!"

Andy Wood, lead pastor of Echo.Church

"I have known Shauna Pilgreen for several years now, and I have watched her and her family since they moved to San Francisco. This book is a great book because of its content. But the book is even better, in my mind, because I have watched Shauna live this out. If you care about people, if you care about God's mission, if you care about people experiencing the love of God and hearing the gospel of Jesus, this book is for you. I hope you will buy it, read it, and live it."

Micah Fries, senior pastor of Brainerd Baptist Church and editor and author of *Islam and North America*

"Most of us know that we're supposed to live as ambassadors for Christ. But if we're honest, few of us have a handle on what that means or looks like on a daily basis. In *Love Where You Live*, Shauna Pilgreen explores the practical realities of living with a 'sent mindset' and opens our eyes to the fact that no matter where we live (whether temporarily or long-term) we're not there by accident. We've been sent here on special assignment."

Larry Osborne, pastor of North Coast Church, Vista, CA, and author

"In this book Shauna teaches us how wonderful and dangerous it is to pray, 'God, I'll go anywhere.' From a small town in Georgia to the heart of San Francisco, Shauna shows us practically what it means to love where you live and see every challenge as an opportunity to share the love of Christ. This book tells the story of how God is using Shauna and her family to impact one of the most culture-defining cities in the world for Christ. Read it and you will be inspired to love where you live!"

Aaron Graham, lead pastor of The District Church, Washington, DC

"Ever so eloquently, Shauna teaches us that God moves us where He chooses based on His perfect plan, not ours. Living sent is not just His desire for us but is also the remedy for the fear and discomfort we may feel when we are sent. Living sent is as joyful and life-giving for us as it is for those God intends we reach and love. This book not only provides practical steps for living our calling but also is a wonderful story that will ease your soul."

Ally Evans, central group leader of NextGen Ministries, Life.Church, Edmond, OK

love
where you
live

HOW *to* LIVE SENT *in*
the PLACE YOU CALL HOME

shauna pilgreen

Revell

a division of Baker Publishing Group
Grand Rapids, Michigan

Published by Revell
a division of Baker Publishing Group
PO Box 6287, Grand Rapids, MI 49516-6287
www.revellbooks.com

Printed in the United States of America

Library of Congress Cataloging-in-Publication Data
Names: Pilgreen, Shauna, 1977– author.
Title: Love where you live : how to live sent in the place you call home / Shauna
    Pilgreen.
Description: Grand Rapids, MI : Revell, a division of Baker Publishing Group,
    [2018] | Includes bibliographical references and index.
Identifiers: LCCN 2018025908 | ISBN 9780800735111 (pbk. : alk. paper)
Subjects: LCSH: Christian life. | Communities—Religious aspects—Christianity. |
    Pilgreen, Shauna, 1977—Anecdotes.
Classification: LCC BV4509.5 .P5655 2018 | DDC 248.4—dc23
LC record available at https://lccn.loc.gov/2018025908

In keeping with biblical principles of creation stewardship, Baker Publishing Group advocates the responsible use of our natural resources. As a member of the Green Press Initiative, our company uses recycled paper when possible. The text paper of this book is composed in part of post-consumer waste.

19   20   21   22   23   24   25   7   6   5   4   3   2

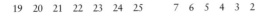

To those with whom I share the sidewalks:
this book is for you.

To the ones I get to hold hands with every day,
Ben, Elijah, Sam, Kavita, and Asher:
this book is because of you.

The Dweller's Prayer

Awaken me, Lord,
to engage with the people around me today.
I choose to make You known
so that Your love may be in them as it is in me.
Come, Jesus. You are welcome here.

Contents

9

Contents

• Part II •

How to Live Sent

• Part III •

The Hope of Living Sent

Foreword

The web of relationships that once dominated the fabric of communities has all but disappeared. Yet each time we hear about it, something within us resonates with it. We have a longing to know our neighbors and have a greater sense of community—even family—with those we live among.

Volumes have been written on what prevents deep community from developing. It's been noted that the loss of the front porch has contributed to the decline of neighbors gathering. Many have developed a "garage door syndrome": the garage door goes up, the car goes in, the garage door goes down. Intruders, also known as the people next door, are kept at a distance.

Another contributing factor is the potential for individuals and families to acquire new jobs, uproot, and start over in a new town that is miles, states, and even continents away. Arguably, people could do this at any point in history. The difference is the ease in which we can now do this and the frequency at which it happens. If you don't like your town or your circumstances, our cultural narrative says, "Move. Change them. Start fresh and live your dream."

As followers of Jesus, we have to ask if that's the narrative we see in Scripture or the narrative we see lived out in Jesus. It doesn't take long to capture a different angle. We are indeed a *sent* people. Our sending, however, is always with a purpose. Abraham and the people of Israel were sent to a promised and specific place. In the covenant community, there were a myriad of laws given on how to take care of one another and welcome the outsider.

When the covenant community was *sent* into exile, as Jeremiah records, God was still sending them with purpose. They were not to decrease or sit idly by. No, the directive from the Lord was to build houses, settle down, plant gardens, eat their produce, marry, have sons and daughters, and give those sons and daughters in marriage so that they can also have sons and daughters (Jeremiah 29:4–6). The higher directive was to "Seek the welfare of the city where I have sent you" (v. 7). Yes, there is activity to be done, but it's driven toward a kingdom purpose.

If anyone has ever been sent with a purpose, Jesus is the perfect embodiment of it. Jesus lived deeply into community. We don't often spend much time thinking about it, as the Gospels do not record those years, but the life of Jesus is a profound example of loving a place. Jesus spent thirty years in a community that was barely a dot on the map of the backwaters of the Roman empire. How many parties did He attend? How many funerals? How much life? How many every-day-in-the-mundane experiences shaped those final three years of ministry? He knew the Jewish law, the customs, the festivals, the rhythms, the people.

He studied. He learned. He, as Eugene Peterson puts it in *The Message*, "became flesh and blood, and moved into the neighborhood" (John 1:14).

· · · · · ·

The people of Israel and the life of Jesus teach us a fundamental value as the people of God in the world: to live intentionally where you have been sent. Know the people and the place. Invest your life deeply, because we are at work bringing pictures of the future kingdom to the here and now.

If this is the better narrative, the narrative the people of God are given to live, the question we need to ask now is, Who is living this narrative, and how do we begin to demonstrate this in our own context? Through her life and the life of her family, Shauna Pilgreen will answer the first question and help you answer the second.

In a deeply inviting and vulnerable way, Shauna invites you into her story, introducing you to the people that make up her immediate and extended family, from a small Southern town to her current urban lifestyle. She gives you the joyous and celebratory experiences and the deeply painful parts as well, because the journey is real and it's not all smooth sailing.

In the pages to come, you'll not only read a compelling story of one family who has chosen to create community rather than run from it but you'll also get some practical, field-level advice for discovering and loving your own neighborhood. You'll get principles to put into practice and tools that will help you see your community, and more of it, in new ways. And you can trust your guide because she's gone before you, lived with purpose, and has the scars and stories to prove it.

It's time to recapture our identity as the *sent* people of God. For some, that identity might involve *going* to a new town, a big city, or even a new country. For all of us, that identity of being sent means "to be sent with a purpose," and to deeply love where we live. May the kingdom break in as we do so.

Randy Frazee, pastor and author of *The Connecting Church*
and *Real Simplicity: Making Room for Life*

Introduction

Why Live Sent?

Hi there. Come on over. Thanks for meeting me here, on the corner of Third and Market. Let's start on the sunny side because I didn't wear enough layers. I see that you left your shades at home. I get it. The day started off quite foggy and cool. Ready to walk? I know you're up for it, or at least are curious, because you picked up this book.

A Welcoming Walk

So, welcome to my city. It probably looks different from yours. Maybe your city is a bit bigger or your town much smaller. I and my fellow citizens of San Francisco are all squeezed into forty-nine square miles. We're known by what neighborhood we live in—the Mission, Portola, Glen Park, Inner Sunset, Outer Sunset, and so on. When I give my address to local friends, I have to give the cross street too. We value good food and celebrate everything. Well, almost everything.

I want you to meet my neighbors. We'll see many while we're out and about. Some will stop by, and others will need us to come to them. Ruth can tell us what it's like to live on these streets we're walking on. Janet has raised her kids here and is now enjoying her grandkids in the very same neighborhood. Rachael and Justin started their family in San Francisco and want to show you how they've jumped in feet-first, learning to love this place. Jordyn is going to join us. Her white cane guides her, but she sees this place better than I do. We're going to peek inside where Darrin works, and you won't be able to miss her big grin from the front desk. Later on we'll stop by for a cup of chai that Israel will gladly serve us. Let me know when you get hungry. I know a great Chinese restaurant near the art museum. The chef, Kathy, will probably stop by our table to tell us what we must eat. And we will order exactly that.

The Sending God at the Intersection

You need to know that, before I moved, I shoved my theology and upbringing into my already overstuffed suitcase, certain they were necessary for my survival. They would be useful for defense and justification and in sharing the gospel if I were asked. I wasn't moving sent. I was moving superior. Yet within hours of arrival into my new home, I quickly noticed that people weren't like me and what I had packed wasn't going to be needed here. Conveniently, a big dumpster was already positioned outside our apartment. Once I tossed my ideals and superiority, I was awakened to see these people and this place with such wide-eyed wonder.

I felt like God tapped me on the shoulder and invited me on a life-altering walk to see the diversity, the brokenness, and the beauty. I looked up and was standing at the crossroads. I could choose to stick to the parts of the Bible that I liked and to keep nearby my files of "what I like to do, how I will spend my time, what works best for me, and the gospel according to my previous culture" or I could pay attention to the God who had sent me here for reasons and a purpose beyond what I could comprehend.

As I looked around, I saw what I had packed was not necessarily what the people needed. I realized I had needs too, and the people pointed me to my greatest need. My life inside the walls of the church was flipped inside out as I became more at home with people who had yet to step inside those walls. I began to see God in the train stations, SROs (Single Room Occupancies, one-room units for residents with minimal income), high-rise apartments, and tech companies. I began to see Him daily in San Francisco, and it was all messy and hard and utterly beautiful. I could see that God didn't fit in a box with rules and regulations. Oh no! I can tell you that He is with Salem on the street and Kay at the abortion clinic and Diane who thinks Someone is up there somewhere. God is moving obstacles that have kept people from walking closer to Him and removing blinders so others might see Him. And I'm getting to be a part of it all. He's rocking my theology of "me" and "them." He's revealing the ugliness in my heart and my daily, hourly, momentary need of the Savior. My heart is still growing in love with the people of my city, because I am choosing to encounter the God of the city—not the god of my theology and ideas.

For where we live is our playground. It is our campus. Our physical location is where we play, imagine, create, explore, unwind, celebrate, dig, and hang upside down. It also contains a people we study, understand, enjoy, consider, ponder, serve, and converse with. And wherever we live, we have a chance to impact and engage with these lives.

Jane Jacobs, a twentieth-century author and activist, was also a housewife and mom with a love for her city of Manhattan that I want to mirror. She thought places were about people. Not buildings. In her words, "Cities have the capability of providing something for everybody, only because, and only when, they are created by everybody."[1] The people I tell you about are important because where we live is not made just of concrete and steel, farmland or factory. It's the people whose heartbeats power our cities and towns.

Yet the reality is that people are constantly moving in and out and around the places we live. Reasons for these moves include family dynamics, housing situations, and career opportunities. Did you know the average American will move eleven times in his or her life? It's common to fixate on the reason for the move rather than God's big picture behind the move. It's time for believers in Jesus Christ to awaken to our reality of being sent, not simply making a move.

Tentmaker Paul talked about God to the leaders in Athens, Greece, when he said,

> The God who made the world and everything in it is the Lord of heaven and earth and does not live in temples built by human hands. And he is not served by human hands, as if he needed anything. Rather, he himself gives everyone life and breath and everything else. From one man he made all the nations, that they should inhabit the whole earth; and he marked out their appointed times in history and the boundaries of their lands. God did this so that they would seek him and perhaps reach out for him and find him, though he is not far from any one of us. (Acts 17:24–27 NIV)

God loves us a whole lot and breathes not only breath in us but a purpose and calling that is as unique as we are. And with that purpose comes a place to dwell. For to dwell is to live, abide, pitch your tent. That dwelling place is strategic.

We downplay God's activity when we see a move simply as a move, or a decision to stay as a commitment to the status quo. Moving is our human explanation for a transition or change in life. Living *sent* is recognizing God's intimate involvement in our lives, whether we are in a new zip code or have been in the same one for years. Living sent aligns our uniqueness to His activity for the purpose of making Him visible to our community. To many He is an unknown God, but to believers He is the sending God.

He sent Abraham. He sent Jonah. He sent out the Twelve. He sent Philip. God has been sending out His people since the beginning. God sent Jesus, right? Of course, Jesus lived sent before He told us to do it. He spent His earthly years living this way. He went into the temple and the synagogues, but he was even more in the fields and the homes and the cities, with the outcasts and those who were attracted to His lifestyle. He said to those closest to Him, "Peace be with you. As the Father has sent me, even so I am sending you" (John 20:21).

Like all Christ followers, we are sent places to show Jesus. Sure, His words are a mission trip verse, but so much more encompassing. They are also a lifestyle that includes how we parent, love, lead, shop, dine, explore, and serve. If we don't show Jesus as we do these things, we will fail the people of our cities and towns and abandon our sending God.

For me, I made a decision on the streets of San Francisco to take His command seriously. To serve and not be served. To consider myself sent and to not consume only but to contribute to the welfare of the city. This wasn't a Wonder Woman moment. It was very much an internal surrender to doing life God's way one day at a time, choosing to be present and awake to the needs and culture around me. I didn't know how it would look. I didn't rally the few local Christians I knew and draw up a battle plan. I took a deep breath, believing I was in San Francisco for a reason beyond myself. And honestly? I could have done all this in the town we lived in before. It wasn't about the move. It was about waking up to God's vision for where I lived.

* * * * * *

So whether you're about to go or you find yourself in an unfamiliar place, or you're wondering what you're still doing *here*— this is your moment, the intersection of life as usual or life as sent. To set this book down and forfeit the adventure or to move forward with God into your city, town, suburb, or neighborhood that needs Him. You might not need a physical relocation but a spiritual relocation of where your heart's affection and mind's attention should be. Let's touch and hear and see and smell and speak His beauty, His Name, and His story.

God has a purpose for our lives where we live. Our career move has greater purpose than just clocking in, leading a team, or winning the case. The business or idea we're intending to start is not to end with going public on Wall Street. The lease of the one-bedroom apartment, the commute, or the countless people at the superstore are not just random pieces of living.

God is calling professionals, families, students, and empty nesters who love Him to specific dwelling places. What each of us has to offer is unique and critical to how God has set up His mission on earth. In the workplace and the neighborhoods, around the conference room and the lunch table, God equips His people with influence and a voice that can speak into the seekers and the lost of cities and towns, suburbs and up-and-coming communities. He expects greatness from His followers. Not a Christian version of life borrowed from the secular market but the finest, most excellent life we can live.

It's dwellers of faith who have the opportunity right now in history to be among the influencers and dreamers. Not as Christians who have moved onto the scene (like I once thought) but as accountants, developers, entrepreneurs, teachers, scientists, lawyers, and volunteers who are Christians. We must have a vision for being where we live. We have to be strategic, creative, and intentional.

Choosing to live sent is moving toward something, not away from something, and leads to an attachment to your community.

Living sent is the strategy of loving people well in your town whom you are sent to love and watching God connect the dots.

Living sent is for those who are called to stay in their childhood places and for those who must cross oceans.

Living sent is for those who want to move and those who have to move. For those who want to stay and those who have to stay.

To live sent is to be tied, first and foremost, to the trinity of the God-created heart, mind, and soul.

Living sent is an awakening to God's activity as we learn a culture and graciously give the truth of Christ.

A Dose of Creativity

Living sent takes His command to go and infuses it with our creativity. It starts with thinking outside the box. Some of you are already there. Others, like me, are Type A, introverted people pleasers who choose neat and tidy over risky and messy any day of the week. Yet this is what blows my mind—thinking outside the box is still within God's creation! Our thinking can never go beyond His thinking, but when we begin to think like He does and see what He sees and respond with His heart, God can take our dreams, ideas, and prayers to unparalleled places. Places where heaven and earth collide and His glory is on display—and an "only God" moment sparks, exploding on earth as it did in heaven.

This lifestyle will lead us to question the voice, influence, and resources God has given us. Know that these were specifically created and given to be used here on earth. They don't travel into eternity. Doing what you were created to do, in your current season of life, in the place you live—this is living sent. To live like you're supposed to be there, not like you're just passing through.

If I can, you can. This is Jesus's model He demonstrated here on earth. He sends us. He makes us all unique. (Not one disciple was like another!) What we bring to the table, paired with what He's already up to, is how He is drawing people to Himself. If we lift Him up, our communities will notice. God wants to take every part of you and use it to tell of Him. Blend it together, and we get to live in this place both confident in Him who sent us and creatively with the gifts and influence He gives. He wants to meet us in our zip code, on our street. He is ready to show us how to live sent in the place we call home.

Dream of the *what ifs* with me.

> What if dwellers who love Jesus become awakened to their purpose in the cities and towns and start living sent?

What if we don't dodge eye contact but offer a smile and an introduction?

What if you were the one who got something started among a few colleagues or neighbors for the simple reason of getting to know one another beyond titles and house numbers?

What if you led the PTA to make a stellar breakfast for the teachers and student body once a week?

What if you hosted the neighborhood Christmas party?

What if you say a private prayer at mealtime that encourages another believer to do the same?

What if you took on the projects no one wanted at an under-resourced school?

What if you invited the interns at your office over for dinner and shared your faith story?

What if you prayed over an area of town and then saw God plant a church there?

What if you were the empty nester looking toward retirement and became the president of the Rotary Club?

What if I tell you that all of these *what ifs* are happening in my corner of the world?!

And here's what will happen as we live sent with creativity:

And this city shall be to me a name of joy, a praise and a glory before all the nations of the earth who shall hear of all the good that I do for them. They shall fear and tremble because of all the good and all the prosperity I provide for it. (Jer. 33:9)

Let Me Be Your Guide

You may be nodding your head, excited to hop on board, but wondering how. It's expected that a guide is a bit of a nerd when it comes to what they love. I'm okay with that. Come with me.

In the pages of this book, I want to show you how and by what means you can reach the people around you every day. I think stories are powerful and will share my experience of moving to and living in San Francisco, as well as stories of friends who are living sent around the world. All of these earthly stories are "to be continued," as we are all a work in progress created to do good works. We'll also explore lives and places in Scripture that radiate this concept. I've got a list of supplies for you to keep on hand and tips for engaging people in conversation. I'm going to show you ways to use your home that include your entire family. Once this becomes a lifestyle, it is addictive. You actually personify a love for the place, and that's attractive to others. This love is genuine because of the work of Christ in you. This will infuse hope for every dweller of faith around you and lead seekers to find Him.

I write to you as a dweller. I show you no statistics but countless stories of His faithfulness. And if God is doing this in San Francisco, He is also doing this in the suburbs of Dallas, in the mountain towns of North Carolina, within the city limits of Detroit, and in your corner of the world. We of all people should laugh the loudest, serve the most, work the best, think the brightest, give the most abundantly, shower His grace the widest, and pray the hardest![2]

This book is best read in the place you call home. I and the baristas in your town highly recommend their coffee shop. Your librarians would be overjoyed to have you at their table. I dare you to read this in your company lounge. Take each chapter and make it the family dinner discussion. It wouldn't surprise me at all if you have a certain place in town that is your thinking spot or respite. Mine is a bench at Walter Haas Park in Diamond Heights that overlooks my city.

· · · · · ·

Thus far you've only needed to read, but I'm about to make a bold move. Throughout the book, you will be given room to doodle and dream, to sketch what you see.

Right here, draw a map of where you live, or tape one inside the cover of this book. If you're going to live sent, you've got to start making marks, and the first ones might as well be in this book. Make sure you label your house and street and anything else that is of importance to you. I will reference this map in other chapters and have you add to it.

Tell me who's leading your community. Take me to the restaurant that is so divine you will return again. I'll be your excuse.

Now, on the next page, dream of what your town can become. Pondering these questions sets your heart toward living sent.

I've written my stories with much prayer for you to dream as you read and take notes as you find yourself in the story God is writing. I'm just one dweller of faith, a red-pinned dot on the map. And so are you. That makes two. And I'm counting on the work of the Spirit to stir your heart toward this lifestyle that will awaken you and those in your home, network, and relationships to live sent. Just as Jesus Christ gave us His stories and showed us how to live in our time here in the places we call home, He left us with this incredible word: "Truly, truly, I say to you, whoever believes in Me will also do the works that I do; and greater works than these will he do, because I am going to the Father" (John 14:12). This is why we live sent. We've got great works to do in the places we are learning to love.

Hannah Whitall Smith wrote in her classic work, *The Christian's Secret of a Happy Life*, that this life of obedience and faith is "so glorious, and human words seem so powerless!" And then she prayed, "May God grant me so to tell it, that every believer to whom this book shall come, may have his eyes opened to see the truth as it is in Jesus, and may be enabled to enter into possession of this glorious life for himself!"[3] I echo this prayer for you, the creatives and dwellers of the places you will call home.

Sketch the skyline.

Include the new construction and the oldest building.

What do you love about your town?

What bothers you?

What would you change?

What seems just right?

Dream of what your town can become.

starting point

• • • • • •

"Jesus said to them again, 'Peace be with you. As the Father has sent me, even so I am sending you.'"

John 20:21

1

The Town of Six Traffic Lights

I'm a rural girl. I was raised among cotton fields and pecan trees, though my father didn't farm. He was and has always been a preacher. When I explain to someone where I grew up, I start with the southeastern portion of the United States. Then I give specifics like Georgia, a coastal state, between South Carolina and Florida. Some people interrupt my progression and infer Atlanta. I give them a look like *Uh, no.* Four hours south of Atlanta, one hour north of Tallahassee, Florida. In a small farming community where the smell of peanuts blows through and where chicken feathers flutter around as the trucks drive from coops to gallows. Where football and hunting are the things in the fall and sweet tea is more popular than water.

But I lost them at Atlanta.

My First Lessons in Living Sent

I didn't learn how to live sent in the city. The concept was first put into practice, again and again, in our town of six traffic lights. Two of the lights were on the Georgia highway that ran through.

29

The other four were around the city square. It was a small town and a good place to grow up.

My family of five—father, mother, two younger sisters, and myself—were the outsiders in this family-rooted town. We stood out because we didn't farm. We stood out because our grandmas, grandpas, aunts, uncles, cousins, and second cousins didn't all live within a twenty-mile radius of the town.

But this didn't keep our community from inviting us into their family gatherings. To gather at their table and let us share their grandparents. And the farmers gave generously of their corn, pecans, peas, beans, cantaloupes, and watermelons. My dad gave of himself as he officiated weddings, visited those in the hospital, and spoke at funerals. This town of six traffic lights wanted a pastor, and we wanted an extended family.

Being new to a place and not having ties afforded us a pair of fresh eyes. And we could see differently with this set of eyes and no family around to keep our calendar full of dinners and celebrations. We could plead the fifth as newcomers within a certain time period (which is determined by the culture in which one lives). And we were considered new for a number of years. I mean, who knew as a fourth-grader wearing her first cheerleading outfit to Football Friday that a pair of bloomers was required? And who knew that a certain boy was your friend's cousin when you kind of mentioned to her that you thought he was cute? Okay, I pleaded the fifth a lot.

"They'll see our out-of-county tags on the car and figure it out." My mother used this excuse more times than I could count. She lived with the mentality that we could always be the new ones around, and that could always be our excuse for doing things a bit differently from all the rest.

My mother was my first teacher in living sent. I thought I was just living my childhood. Once, in grade school, the girls in their ballet outfits asked me where I was going. I didn't dare tell them the nursing home. I played it cool with my bag of Funyuns and Crystal Pepsi in my hands at the Stop-n-Shop.

"I don't know—something fun—not sure though—see ya."

But I knew it was the nursing home we were going to. My sisters and I did "normal kid activities" like basketball and piano lessons too. But we also routinely walked up the steps and into the sterile and sweet community of elderly people who beamed to have us there. We would practice our piano before this audience and get rave reviews.

Living sent also took us to the other side of the train tracks. Several girls helped with childcare at our church and they would sometimes need a ride home. They didn't live like we lived and we didn't live like they lived. They raised pigs in their backyard and would graduate at the very top of their classes. Brilliant girls. Brilliant. We attempted to breed English bulldogs in our backyard and strived to have the smarts these girls did. We tried. We really tried.

Living sent looked like sitting around our dining room table with missionaries and pastors who were in town for revival services. Miss Margaret would teach us the songs she would sing to the children of Liberia about lifting Jesus higher and stomping Satan lower. With hand and foot motions, of course. Other missionaries would share what seemed like the stuff movies are made of about how they were persecuted and robbed and cursed. Then their faces would shine like the sun as they told story after story of going into the dark places and sharing Jesus with the witch doctors and witnessing healing and life transformation. Stories of starting churches and growing food and learning from the locals. I could see it in their eyes. My soul was drawn to what they were experiencing in Africa. They weren't relaxing in the status quo. Even as a child, I had seen enough to make a decision about my future. America wasn't their home anymore. They were living sent in other parts of the world, and I wanted to as well.

It was in the sports arena where my pastor-dad lived sent; he became chaplain for a couple of athletic teams. In the town of six traffic lights, race was a difference maker. Skin color made a difference in where one lived and went to school, church, and work, but it didn't matter as much on the sports field. Dad exchanged the pulpit and his preacher voice for locker rooms and pep talks—all to build relationships across racial lines that weren't happening in many other places in town on Friday nights.

We didn't have traditions in this new place. We would create them. My family wasn't tied down to everyone else's schedules. We didn't know the backstory. We didn't know the gossip (yet). We hadn't figured out who was related to whom. We hadn't learned that the beach was *the* vacation spot and that the size of Christmas depended upon how good the crops were that year. We just didn't know. We were new to the town of six traffic lights.

Abraham was new to the town of Canaan. In Hebrews 11:8–10 we read,

> By faith Abraham, when called to go to a place he would later receive as his inheritance, obeyed and went, even though he did not know where he was going. By faith he made his home in the promised land like a stranger in a foreign country; he lived in tents, as did Isaac and Jacob, who were heirs with him of the same promise. For he was looking forward to the city with foundations, whose architect and builder is God. (NIV)

God told him to leave his country, his people, and his family and go "to the land that I will show you." How's that for vagueness? That makes the town of six traffic lights sound absolutely specific.

It Takes Faith to Move

When God calls, faith should be our response. This is true even when the call from God is a new way of looking at the world right where we are. For Abraham, he had only known life with his extended family in the same geographic region. If Abraham had stayed in the place that was familiar, he wouldn't have exercised the same amount of faith it took to move. Whenever we are called to leave the familiar for the unknown and uncertain, our faith is tested. And faith is not what you can see but what you can't see. Faith is the heart response. Obedience is the physical response. Faith says, "Yes, God." Obedience is one foot, then another. We follow not because of where He's leading or who else will be there or what we can expect but because it's God and He alone is worth following.

By faith we move. My family has had to believe God for what we couldn't see and make steps into uncharted waters. And the tricky part about faith is that because it's invisible, it's hard to paint the picture of what we've been asked to do for those around us. That is why we have to be certain of the calling.

The Calling Has to Be Present

Some days all we have is our calling. The new place will be hard. Our outlook will get foggy. Our hearts will grow heavy. People will let us down. Circumstances will change. Knowing God has called us to this place will make all the difference in those moments. To clarify the calling, let's ask the right questions. They flow from God, not from this fleeting, always-changing world.

- Is God first?
- Do I love Him more than work, culture, success, and location?
- Is our move about more than what we can get out of it?
- Is it possible He's got a plan for us here?
- If He is my hope, will I share Him?

If we cannot answer yes to these questions, then when the physical location stops doing it for us, we will bail.

Not long after we moved, I remember asking my mom the wrong question: "Does a bus come to the town of six traffic lights?" I wanted to get on the bus back to where we used to live. We never did—partly because a bus didn't come by in the town of six traffic lights. But mostly because I knew we were supposed to be there. The calling was present. It was visible in my parents, and I couldn't deny the peace in my heart.

Abraham was the first one officially called in the Scriptures. His call from God didn't include his future destination but the move from where Abraham was presently.

I'd like to think if God had told me everything on one of those days I sat on the front porch waiting for a bus to come by, He would have said something like this: "Shauna, for now you live in the town of six traffic lights. When you leave, you will not return here but will take with you what you've learned. I am sending you to the city of San Francisco. The people will point out your Southern dialect and marvel at the number of children you have. You'll find yourself surprised most days that this will be your home. Your life will intersect with the masses on a daily basis. Be My mouthpiece. Be My hands. Show compassion. I will go before you and still have many things to teach you, show you, and shape in you. It won't be easy, but I who call you am faithful."

Our calling God is a sending God, from Abraham forward. God sent the Israelites as exiles into Babylon. They didn't haphazardly end up there. We don't feel sorry for Abraham but rather learn from his calling. We don't have to take pity on the exiles either. Most people don't feel sorry for us when they learn we live in San Francisco. For when we see ourselves as sent, when we are called, it's a joy. An absolute joy!

Sink Roots Down

In Abraham's day it wasn't common for people to leave their homeland. It wasn't common in my day either, in the town of six traffic lights. By faith, Abraham made his home in a very different place, which means he didn't see it as temporary. We are to make our home in the places God calls us. If we see our move as a "stop along the way," we will be waiting for the bus to come by, and on hard days we will hop on it. Be sure of it. Rather, put things up on the walls. Break down those cardboard boxes for someone else to use. Embrace the reality that you are a citizen of this physical place.

Keep in mind we will be "strangers in a foreign land" this side of heaven because we are ultimately citizens of God's kingdom. Opportunities will arise, and we'll want to run away from the craziness of this place, but instead let's run toward the calling of living here. The nation was different because Abraham said yes to the calling and made Canaan his home. Our places can be different because we say yes to the call God has for us to live sent here.

I grew up quoting Jeremiah 29:11, "For I know the plans I have for you, declares the LORD," in regard to happiness and health. But when we study this verse in its context, we can see God was saying to the Israelites, "Hey, I know you are in exile in Babylon, but while you are living in a city that is not your home, in a city that has very different foundational beliefs than yours, stay there, live at peace with those around you, and keep at the center that I am your God." It's as if God is our real estate agent, helping us settle in. God always says it well.

Live Forward Thinking

Wherever we live, we do so because God has called us and believes we can make the most eternal impact there. The language we use among our church family in San Francisco is that we leverage the temporary for the sake of the eternal. God could change my calling or any of our callings. But, as best as we understand things, it seems that my family can make the most eternal impact and best influence the future and the globe by having San Francisco as our home base. The stories that flow through the pages of this book are all a result of a call, a heart response that led to a "one foot in front of the other" response.

The reason Abraham was able to move by faith, recognize his calling, and sink down roots is because he was looking ahead.

35

He saw the big picture. It wasn't simply about a move but about being sent and living sent. Looking forward affords us the grand view. To see the city. To see our move. To see potential. To see opportunity. To fix our eyes on heaven, on our faith being made sight once and for all.

The Starting Point

We can start from anywhere and come from everywhere. The rural life. The urban life. The childhood in the pews. The childhood on the streets. It's a faulty theory that our upbringing has to be our future. A stagnant culture tends to tie our destiny to our parents' occupations and dreams. This same culture tries to dictate the boundaries in which we process life and our world. Even the church in a stagnant place can box God in and stifle the next generation's pursuit of God.

But God can speak to us at any age and in any setting. Whatever our past experiences, God has a creative way of weaving them into our present reality and our future destinations. He doesn't see our past, present, and future contained within orderly, white-bordered frames. He sees our lives collectively fitting together, working together.

He takes our wonderings, doubts, detours, mistakes, successes, failures, and everything else and uses it for His good. Let Paul remind us. Romans 8:28 says that "we know that for those who love God all things work together for good, for those who are called according to his purpose."

He can work despite where we've come from. He uses the weak to confound the wise. He used David, a boy from the pasture, to get the attention of the entire Philistine army. He sent royal Moses out to the wilderness then back to royalty. He called Peter. He sent Paul. I'm guessing you're expecting me to bring up Mary next. Sure. He found Mary, a teenage girl. How old was Josiah when he was crowned king? God can't be pegged down to one way of doing something.

We've got to revisit who we are and where He's brought us to better understand how He wants to use us. It's hard to fathom how I could be used in the city, considering my "average" story. But once I got specific about my life, I realized the city I live in doesn't have a high percentage of Southern stay-at-home moms who write while married to a pastor with kids in the public schools. Maybe I'm not so average. And God has a specific use for each part of your story. Get specific about who you are and what brought you here. This is the starting point.

Take the example of the recently married MIT graduate who gets a job at a popular law firm. He and his wife buy an apartment and start their careers. Then they start a family and learn to coordinate their schedules to get the kids to school and activities. He is now a father and husband who practices law and engages with the people in his condominium complex.

How about the creative free spirit drawn to downtown with a dream and just enough money to begin? She enters wide-eyed to the possibilities of honing her crafts of photography and visual arts. With flexible hours and a growing brand, she now thrives by using her God-given gifts where she once only dreamed of living.

Or what about the millennial who makes her first move away from home to take a teaching position at a new school? She steps into an environment of tenured teachers yet believes she has something to offer that is new and fresh, while displaying a teachable and respectful heart. That's the starting point.

* * * * * *

My family lived in the town of six traffic lights for thirteen years. The locals, with their deep family roots, loved us and invited us in. Mrs. Hazel Collins, who was related to everybody, taught me how to pray and let me climb her magnolia tree. One of the ballerinas and I spent hours studying together at the library. My sisters and I played in the city softball league with girls of color. Unfortunately, I didn't put in the practice on the keys and can't play the piano today (my apologies to Mrs. Mary Collins. Yes, they're related). I even got married in the church in the city square.

My wedding day was my last day to call the town of six traffic lights home. With my husband, who was from a town of dozens of traffic lights, I would live in several places in our first years of marriage. Those childhood years I was storing up images and experiences of living sent subconsciously.

DWELLER TIP

Leave the door open in the apartment complex while cooking dinner. Even if the dog leads the way, his owner will have to have a conversation!

—Keel family, dog owners

2

The Comfortable Life

We were living the good life in the Midwest. It was comfortable, affordable, sustainable, breathable—and safe. The community was hidden in the shadow of the Ozark mountains, nestled among rivers and lakes. Our home mimicked the other twenty or so in the neighborhood.

Grass was in abundance in the front and back yards. Our kids toddled around and picked up baseball basics, from hitting off a tee to learning the order of the bases. Sprinklers kept the grass its intended color and created hours of free playtime that led to a glorious concept called naps.

Our garage could hold two cars and our lives warranted them both. Car A typically toted children, groceries, strollers, booster seats, sports equipment, and park essentials. Well, Car B did the same, come to think of it. But one car did go to work and the other stayed closer to home. Work and home were an easy twenty minutes apart. Two cars were convenient, and besides, everybody else was doing it.

Our days consisted of church life, little kids, church life with little kids, and free time with people who had little kids. We spent lots of time with a neighboring family who also went to our church and became very close friends. We'd barbecue together, and Ben would tell funny stories in exchange for the husband's expertise on lawn care and Home Depot tips. We learned to build in date nights as a couple and often did double dates with those neighbors.

I'd wonder about our other neighbors, who were doing yard-work on Sundays, and voice a prayer for them as I left my two-car garage for church. One time I invited them to our church, but they already had one.

Our church was thriving and missional. Most Sundays we were sending a short-term team across the ocean, praying over volunteers going across town, or commissioning a couple to a career in missions. Ben served under the leadership of a sincere and shepherding pastor. Our kids learned about Jesus through dramas, small groups, colorful classrooms, and weekly programming.

The community had all we needed to live comfortably. Life was good. Almost too good.

When Comfort Is Treasured above All Else, We Have Made It an Idol

To live sent, comfort has to go. And not go with you. Now, don't get me wrong. Comfort has its perks. We eat to feel comfortable. We buy the necessary furniture to sleep and lounge comfortably. We dress as comfortably as we can. Comfort feels good, tastes good, sounds good. La-Z-Boy has a slogan: "live life comfortably." As they should. They sell furniture.

We live by a slogan whether we advertise it or not. Set life up for comfort. Get the salary up to a cushioned place. Relax in that chair with retirement in view. Buy that bigger house to hold it all. While we may have to work hard to live comfortably, we don't have to work to love what's comfortable. Yoga pants, macaroni and cheese, and sunshine. Six-figure salaries, vacation destinations, and delivery of books, food, and dry cleaning to your front door. Comfort is just that, though—comfort. And comfort can be dangerously desensitizing.

As I typed these words, my middle son, Sam, read them over my shoulder and asked me what I meant by them.

"Sam, can you imagine what life is like in Mosul tonight for a kid your age or a woman my age?"

As he shook his head, my heart ate my own words. Neither of us could. We lay cuddled up on the bed watching On Demand TV, surrounded by pillows and blankets with the soft ambience of a lamp. We weren't concerned for our safety or what was outside our window. Our bellies were full and our bodies were clean.

Now, for Sam, and I hope for myself, we have started to see how often we've become desensitized because of our comfort. Comfort can be cunning and sneak into first place, resulting in idolatry.

Jeremiah the prophet warned the Israelites concerning the idolatry of comfort. They needed to "know and see that it is evil and bitter for you to forsake the LORD your God; the fear of me is not in you, declares the Lord GOD of hosts" (Jer. 2:19). God is the Giver of comfort, but I can't find where He advocates for comfortability. He is a jealous God in wanting to be Who we long for most. Little materialistic gods of comfort were never meant to take His place.

Jonah should know. He ran from his calling. Oh, if he could have only seen it would lead to days in the belly of a big fish. It was in that uncomfortable belly that Jonah uttered these words: "Those who pay regard to vain idols forsake their hope of steadfast love" (Jon. 2:8). He wasn't begging God for a day at the spa or a night at the Hilton. He recognized that nothing but God could satisfy. And while we don't have to work to love what's comfortable, we do have to work to love those places and people that are hard to love and understand. Jonah got that too. (Hello, Nineveh!) When we let the pursuit of comfort go, we can see clearer our calling— for comfort is to be seen as a gift, not a destination.

When Comfort Is Seen as a Destination, We Have Made It a Life of Its Own

A life of comfort is called a win for the enemy. Once we make Christ our Lord, Satan has lost one battle. His next battle is to keep us comfortable so that we fail our earthly mission. We are to live out of our calling, not our comfort. A life of comfort can keep us from our purpose. It can benefit and aid our purpose and be used for God's glory, but it was never intended to be the point of life. Living comfortably causes us to miss out on the heart of God.

I like comfort—very much so. I'm writing this sentence, and probably only this sentence, on a plane to Hawaii, a trip for both work and pleasure. When we seek comfort, intentionally or subconsciously, we settle in, take the reins of life, and make self and safety supreme.

I was on the verge of making comfort my goal in the good life in the Midwest, but comfort can be found in the urban setting as well. The city has all the movie feels. Espresso with a friend at a cafe table. Romantic dinners on hidden back patios. Antique elevators to a third floor of an apartment building. The businessperson swinging open a glass door of a high-rise with briefcase in hand, off to the next big deal. A couple hailing a taxi after a night at the theater. But eventually the newness wears off and the city wears you out. The comforts of the past sparkle on social media, and the phone call with Grandma somehow carries her particular and distinctive smell. If we move for comfort, we will always be moving and buying and selling and searching, satisfied only temporarily.

What I didn't know in the Midwest is that the best was yet to come. This had nothing to do with what *I* was setting up. It had everything to do with what God was orchestrating. And it would only happen after we let comfort go and pursued the abundant life God was preparing for us. He was using the town of six traffic lights and the comfortable life in the Midwest to launch my family into the city, where we would gladly give up comfort for creativity.

We Are to See Comfort as a Gift, Not a Get

So, God didn't design life to be comfortable, but He is so gracious in giving us tastes of comfort. A taste of comfort is called *rest*. A missionary will call this a *furlough*. A professor will call this a *sabbatical*. Christians call it *Sabbath*. We tend to call these rests *vacations*, weekend getaways. But it's a ridiculous notion that God would give us a life of vacation and we would only occasionally work. He designed us as workers. We are created to strive for excellence, to learn and struggle. We take breaks from our work.

In the same light, He gives us tastes of comfort in our calling. I've had some of the best fried chicken in the restaurants of San Francisco. Every time I pass a magnolia tree in the city, I can't help but think of Mrs. Hazel teaching me to pray. I journey to the South every June to swat gnats and walk barefoot in the grass. That speaks comfort to me. What speaks comfort to you?

The voice of God was the greatest comfort to us in the Midwest. Ben and I would say that we heard the voice of God more clearly there than in the hustle and bustle of our previous position. I look back at our comfortable life and call it our oasis. God was using that time to lay a foundation of what we would need for what He was about to call us to. We drank from the well and got full. We were about to be spilled out. I'll let David say it to us, as he did it best in one of his many songs:

> Some wandered in desert wastes,
>   finding no way to a city to dwell in;
> hungry and thirsty,
>   their soul fainted within them.
> Then they cried to the LORD in their trouble,
>   and he delivered them from their distress.
> He led them by a straight way
>   till they reached a city to dwell in.
> Let them thank the LORD for his steadfast love,
>   for his wondrous works to the children of man!

43

For he satisfies the longing soul,
> and the hungry soul he fills with good things.
> (Ps. 107:4–9)

The gift of comfort can be best received with the discipline to trust and obey God with everything. My friend Ginger and I talked about this over coffee and bagels one morning in the Midwest. She didn't hesitate to tell me it would be harder for her to stay and resist the idol of comfort, where the line is blurry, than pack up like me and move to a place where it would be clearly distinct. But she would stay and I would go, for we both could attest to the work of God firsthand in our lives, and it was far greater to be a part of it rather than just hear about it. Comfort and this lifestyle weren't about location; they were about perspective. For it would be years from this moment that her family would give up an established career packed with travel perks and prestige, forsaking comfort and security to walk into God's next thing for them. And they experienced all of this without ever leaving town.

What's the worst thing that could happen if we make comfort supreme? We might never fulfill God's mission for our lives. We pass this shadow mission down to our children: *Kids, our mission in life is to set you up comfortably, protect you, and live life safe.* We miss out on God's richest blessings, which far outweigh what any earthly comfort can afford.

What's the best thing that can happen by letting comfort go? It's the very answer we would be able to give our little boys in the months that followed our decision to move to San Francisco: *Kids, our mission in life is to love you well and take you with us as we follow God by faith in taking risks that lead to others knowing Him.*

But I wasn't saying this quite yet. I was enjoying the comfortable life.

DWELLER TIP

Living sent is just as much embracing your new culture as it is removing the tag of your car from your previous culture!

—Team Rozmus, Austin, Texas,
transplants from Tennessee

3

Thanks, Queen Esther

We were just months into our good Midwestern life when Ben started teaching on the life of Esther. As queen, she was in a plush position to leverage her life for the sake of others. Of course, the position didn't feel so plush when she realized her entire people group was about to be annihilated and she had to approach the king about it. With the help of outsider information, she found herself facing a life-changing decision. It was a moment to be risky, daring, and brave. A moment to say, "It's not all about me, but about us." But Queen Esther said it more eloquently: "And if I perish, I perish" (Esther 4:16). If she didn't do something, who would? The man on the outside had done his part. She had won favor with the king. Yet evil was winning. It was her time to go—to play her part.

Ben swallowed the very words God had given him for this teaching series as he spoke to our church. It was a challenge for him. Challenges can be presented "in your face" or they can start with a stir, move to an urge or prompting, then wreck the soul. I think that God was gradually using Esther's life to challenge Ben. He let this stirring simmer in his own heart before approaching me with it.

When Ben and I knew we would marry, we agreed to chase God anywhere around the world. (I even have a glass globe that sits on an etched base and proclaims this vision of ours.) Now, Ben did what any respectable husband would do. He asked me to pray about it. It didn't affect just him anymore but also me and the kids. In his soul, he was certain he was hearing God calling us to make a risky move to start a church in an unreached city in America. *What? Huh?* In the moment, I forgot about our agreement. We had just arrived in April, and he had prepared the Esther series through the summer and started teaching it in November. I'm pretty sure we still had a few boxes to unpack. Our oldest child was five, and we had already toured the high school where he would play baseball! It wasn't time to go.

So I took this to the source of all the commotion. "God, I thought I heard 'Africa' when I was a fourth grader. I don't recall us talking about great American cities." Well, I had been ten years old at the time. Maybe my recall was a bit blurry.

I took the next ten days to pray about it—amid normal life with three littles. My prayers weren't long or deep. But they were raw, and His peace was clear. Ben and I knew others could come and do the job of being a teaching pastor of a thriving missional church in the Midwest, but the call for unreached, strategic cities? That call was for us.

There was nothing plush about this new assignment. After the decision was made, I was already quoting Esther, with whom I had a love-hate relationship at this point: "If I perish, I perish."

I came into this world with little equipment for adventure but plenty for planning. And since opposites attract, Ben was leading the adventure and I was right beside him with a clipboard and a spreadsheet. He began to strategize about US cities. He narrowed it down to five cities where churches were few or nonexistent and where change was innovative and world-shaping. From his research, these were Chicago, Boston, San Diego, San Francisco, and New York. We weren't keenly aware of church planting networks at the time. It was more of talking to *this* person who knew of someone who kind of had a connection with *that* person who might use the phrase "church planting." There was this search engine called Google, and we used it often—Ben for research, while I stared at the map components, very aware of the distance from here to there and the street views that were not like my current street views.

I really thought God needed us on the East Coast. *Oh, the East Coast is so lovely in the fall. The history is rich and vast. The time zone is the same as my family's.* I might have told Ben a time or two that I heard this from God. But countless people approached Ben to put him in hypothetical scenarios about San Francisco. The Bay Area church-planting strategist was the one to return his phone calls and emails.

So we gave our research over to God. He didn't need it, but it was an act of worship to say we did our part and would step back and watch Him do His. Ben called a few friends who might be interested in pursuing this with us.

A fifty-day prayer guide was drawn up at the end of November—just weeks after God used Esther to wreck our world. The friends who agreed to go with us joined in the prayer. We made our initial visit to San Francisco on the fiftieth day.

In our four days spent in the Bay Area, we planned to make San Francisco the tourist day before getting down to the business of prayerfully considering the nearby locales of Palo Alto, Emeryville, Mountain View, and places in between. San Francisco seemed "too city," and moving anywhere near there would still be considered a sacrifice on our part out of obedience to God. On the last night, we drove down to San Jose to have dinner with the staff of a church plant that was a year old. Before we got there, the conversation became heated, and we were forced to pull the car over in a random industrial park. The setting was not important. The conversation was.

Everyone surprised each other. We were all saying the same thing. Then we weren't saying anything. Could it be? Unanimous yeses to plant a church in downtown San Francisco? My reasoning was this: if we were giving up the good life in the Midwest for life among the unchurched in the city, then the suburbs wouldn't suffice. We had to step out of our new home every day well aware of our purpose. We had to walk the streets with those who might come to our church. We had to exchange comfort for calling. A move to the suburbs would be a bit of an adjustment, but then I'd get cozy again. I didn't want that. God had done too much of a stir to move me from comfort to the unknown. I wanted to feel this move. I'd feel it among the tall buildings and the endless stretches of sidewalks. Our kids would too. It was the city we were called to, and it would be to the city we would go.

Then our airplane landed back in the Midwest. Fresh air was in abundance, and so was the expanse of grass. As we drove home, I recalled the recent afternoon we had spent driving through San Francisco in the rain. Ben had asked if there was anything else we wanted to see, and I sheepishly requested green space. We drove around a park's perimeter among the tech offices in the SoMa neighborhood. *Has the city occupied every square inch but this tiny spot?* I knew we hadn't seen it all, but this was measly. It was my Queen Esther moment to say, "It's not all about me, but about us." We could play on that playground. We could meet the neighbors. We could make this work. But it was easier to tell myself this while back in the Midwest.

In the coming days, my soul was wrecked over and over again. It was no longer Queen Esther's fault. It was the very stirring that started in the fourth grade, that urged me into a marriage partnership with an "outside the box" thinker, and that was now soul-transforming.

Once the word was out that we were moving after only being in the Midwest for a year, I started to get excited. Many were thrilled that we were pursuing God in the city. These people would be some of our finest cheerleaders. But there's always a handful of others. Those other voices always seem louder, somehow.

"You know San Francisco is on the San Andreas fault line, right?"

"You're headed to Sodom and Gomorrah!"

These other voices questioned if we had heard God clearly. Actually, they were convinced we hadn't. I get it. We were barely thirty with three little boys. We hadn't done anything like this before. I'm sure our Midwest church expected us to stick around longer than a year.

I often came back to the stirring, the urging, the transforming. The voices outside of me couldn't derail the Voice inside of me.

The Stirring

God uses our past, our upbringing, and our experiences to stir our hearts for what stirs His. He takes that mission trip overseas to open your eyes to see the very thing that is taking place in your own zip code. I use the word *stir* because that's what it feels like internally. He's got that wooden spoon hitting the corners of your heart.

Mary pondered it in her heart. She could tell us what the stirring felt like. Elizabeth felt it in her belly. We both know that David had to feel it on those days spent under the shade tree as a shepherd after he had already been anointed as king but wasn't quite living like one yet. Samuel kept getting up at night, certain his name was being called. Philip sensed the man in the chariot wanted to chat. God is not mentioned in the book of Esther, but His activity is all around. God might not be the Name above all Names in your city, but His activity is all around. His stirring. His presence.

The Urging

Are you wondering if you're supposed to act? When that stirring becomes an urging, pay attention. God's just getting started with what He's about to unleash. God doesn't tell us everything—for obvious reasons. We'd freak out. Think about Esther. I guarantee when she was playing princess with her friends as a girl, she wasn't thinking it would really come true. When she was orphaned then raised by her uncle, she probably wasn't expecting she would one day help her entire Jewish family. Even when Esther did make it into the palace, she was only one of many beautiful women being considered. As her story progressed and she became queen, it wasn't often that the king called for her.

The urge in my childhood church felt like a racing heart and clammy hands clamped on the pew in front of me, prompting me to go to the altar to pray or make a public decision. The urge in my "slightly grown-up heart" felt like a rope pull toward something greater than myself. Urges aren't necessarily clarity but undeniably the Holy Spirit doing the work of the Father in us.

We humans specialize in hindsight. Our backward 20/20 vision is spot on. After it all unfolds, we get it. But it's in the urging that we lean in rather than away. We're hearing the voice of God and are in the tension of the decision. And that prompting toward faith is Him.

The Transforming

That first step is you. That next step revealed is Him. It's a dance, really. Not that I know much about dancing, growing up as a Baptist girl. You can imagine what it was like for me to dance with my Baptist pastor dad for the first time at the age of thirty-nine. Such freedom twirled around the room when he asked me to dance at my cousin's wedding in the north Georgia mountains.

Transformation ushers in freedom. It unleashes. Freedom isn't felt in chains but in the break. Comfort traps. Conformity ties the hands together. But transformation is a thorough and dramatic change.

We're not the same anymore. And it's visible. The old has gone, the new has come. The caterpillar is no more. What is real is the butterfly, because transformation is metamorphosis. God does this to build something new in us. And it isn't going to be what has always been. Transformation is reconstructive. It's the idea of stripping away what might have worked before but doesn't work now. It's not a fresh coat of paint or rearranging of furniture. Our life blueprints are surrendered for His pleasing and perfect plan.

My family's call to the city was a career move—a dramatic change. We would take into account our kids and leaving family and the familiar. Yet for all believers, the call is always deeper. When that is received, the stirring, the urging, and the transforming make sense. Author Philip Yancey asked it like this: "What is faith, after all, but believing in advance what will only make sense in reverse?"[1]

As I looked back from the comfortable life to the town of six traffic lights, I had told God, *I'll go anywhere.* I'd pictured African huts, French marketplaces, Asian villages. However, raising kids and living close to family was warm, cozy, and convenient. The move to the Midwest made sense, even apart from God's leading, for we started building health into our marriage and family. So when God called us to San Francisco, I knew this would be the giving back of the very gift God had given me years ago—to give Him my *I'll go anywhere.* When God gives us abundant life, He wants us to live it. When God gifts us an income, He wants us to steward it well. When God provides direction, He wants us to go.

Abraham was asked to give back the very gift God had given him, the gift of Isaac. I was asked to give back the very gift God had given me. San Francisco, not Africa? West Coast, not the East Coast? City center, not the suburbs? High rise, not acreage?

Esther's story intersected with mine as we knew we were to move to San Francisco. This was a strategic city and would require some risks. We stepped forward in faith, not sure of what was ahead but ready to start.

DWELLER TIP

In each place I have lived, there have been important cultural norms that become the guide on how to live. Though they vary, God's Word remains the same. The fun part lies in that, since we are all wired differently, what He asks of us varies.

—Gabriela Kropf, Ecuadorian living in Brooklyn, New York

4

Start to Stay

Ben was motivated like I had never seen before. He traveled across Missouri and neighboring states to tell pastors what we were going to do, reached out over the phone, and worked on finding the networkers, supporters, and financial backers we needed to establish a new church in San Francisco. We were, in the language of the affluent and influential West Coast city we were moving to, a "start-up." That meant a hefty budget, a launch team, a location, a prospectus, and some believers in an entity that didn't yet exist—but had been growing ever since Pentecost.

Ben did the start-up thing and I did the get-rid-of-things. To transition from our comfortable life in the Midwest with its two-car garage to a high-rise apartment in the city center, we sold at least half of our possessions, gifted one of our cars to a family member, got rid of all our major appliances, and slimmed down on the kids' indoor and outdoor toys. We sold our larger-than-life bedroom set, and would sell our souls to IKEA once we arrived. I say "sell our souls" because it would take our Craigslist money, our marriage, our time we could have been using to start a church, and all of our patience to assemble our new urban furniture.

On one of our visits to San Francisco, we found the Craigslist headquarters and I soon began to live on Craigslist—looking for a place to live and for all the items we needed. If I wasn't on Craigslist, I was on the *San Francisco Chronicle* website, learning about the local festivals, foods, developments, and sports, and I also became addicted to blogs that took on every angle involved in the lottery system for getting our kids into a good school in the city.

In the midst of all the planning and preparing, Ben and I made a list of nonnegotiables—what we refused to give up versus what we could give up. We could give up a second car and owning a home. We could give up having extended family and our strong network of ministry close by. But we refused to sacrifice our marriage or our children. We were more committed than ever as we walked into these uncharted waters. We were also going to hold our kids' hands along the way. They wouldn't follow us but join us. We needed their perspective and influence. This was a "together" endeavor.

It was the hardest telling our oldest son, Elijah, a kindergartner at the time, that he would not be returning to his school the next year. I had to get reassurance from God with this particular issue that we were indeed moving.

For spring break, we took the boys to their new home. I enjoyed having them along, and it became more real as I saw it through their little eyes. On our first two trips we had looked at the city from the vantage point of starting a church. This trip was different. We took the out-of-towner approach and threw ourselves into everything touristy. We rode the cable cars. We sampled Ghirardelli chocolate. We ate clam chowder in bread bowls at Fisherman's Wharf and drove across the Golden Gate Bridge. We stuck our toes in the cold Pacific.

The boys saw it as a great adventure. They had nothing to lose and everything to gain. Their minimal packing lists included Mom, Dad, favorite stuffed animals, LEGOs, and baseball gloves. Since those were easy yeses, they were all in.

A few short months and many hugs and farewells later, we were ready as could be. The moving truck was packed, and Ben and some dedicated friends headed west. I took the faster route via the friendly skies with the three kids, promising Ben I would indeed arrive on the West Coast.

. . . . . .

Everything arrived when we moved to San Francisco. Everything except my heart. I was mentally prepared for the move west and thought my heart had been part of the many conversations. Yet nothing can adequately prepare that blood-pumping, oxygen-giving organ for a transplant to a new place. God designed it to be the wellspring of life. The heart has to experience something, not simply be told about it. My heart and mind had to be tethered together for this to happen, and while I could recite my new address, my heart wasn't feeling at home yet. This "starting" thing was harder than I had planned.

That was made perfectly clear as I walked the streets and paid attention to everyone else in my new home. I wasn't a career woman like most. I wasn't an au pair like some. I wasn't even a part-time employee for a company that allowed me to work from anywhere in the world. These unnerving realities would thrust me against the back side of my front door as I escaped the noises outside and turned inward. *Who am I? Oh, yes. That's who I am.* And it felt intrinsically unique and lonely.

More times than not, we think we're the only ones who have our specific role, and that's mostly true. I'm married to a pastor. I am a writer. I have a big family according to urban standards. And if those don't come with a stigma, I even have a Southern accent. It has fizzled quite a lot, in my opinion. Ben begs to differ. It escalates if I'm talking on the phone with my mother or when it's way past my bedtime. At first I tried to hide it, but as I saw my Asian neighbors chatting with one another in Cantonese, and my Latino neighbors conversing, I realized who I am was a gift, not a handicap. There is no one like you and me, and that's how God designed His creation. So, we start with who we are.

Maria Goff, a San Diego dweller and author of *Love Lives Here*, writes,

> We all start by starting. It's usually the first step that's the hardest. You raise a hand. You admit the problem. You ask for help. You tie the knot. You start climbing. Everything after starting is just making the next move. . . . We start over in our lives . . . we'll make it a holy place again, nothing more and nothing less. . . . And for the courageous at heart, we simply start again.[1]

Starting to stay is the first step. Choosing to stay will be what happens each day forward. Every time I venture back to Georgia and spend time with my extended family, I see what I'm missing out on. I see my nieces and nephews growing up and the handiwork my father has done at my sister's house. I see the price of gasoline and the myriad of drive-thrus. I hear of celebrations I missed. Yet something powerful also happens. I realize that where I am living has a stronger pull on my soul than where I could be living.

A fear of missing out is not from God. He wants us to stay in our lane, in our place He has for us, doing what He's called us to do. A fear of missing out surfaces from comparison and competition. It's a survival tactic, not a staying power. Most of us can live anywhere. This journey is for those who want to live in the place God has for us.

It's the only place we can begin. And yes, starting is scary—but necessary. God uses our starting point. He knows it better than anyone else. He knows where we've come from and where we want to go. He knows who we've been in the past and who we want to become.

Besides, we don't want to go anywhere without God, for it's His going with us that gives us favor and distinction. With Moses, the Lord replied, "My presence will go with you, and I will give you rest" (Exod. 33:14). Then Moses said to him, "If your presence will not go with me, do not bring us up from here" (v. 15).

I was now living in a city referred to as "the graveyard for church plants." I was among sprawling hills and thick wintry fog over the summer months. I knew the statistic that there were more dogs than kids in the city, even though our family adjusted it a bit. My new place was the second most densely populated American city, after Manhattan. Ben and I couldn't get our minds around a budget as we were now living in the most expensive place in America. If we weren't careful, our minds would roam back to "Previousville," and that's not where we lived anymore. My head was saying we should go where

the grass was greener,

the sunshine was brighter,

the mortgage was cheaper,

the people were friendlier,

the hours were less grueling,

the traffic was lighter,

the state was more blue or more red,

the schools were ranked higher,

the walkability score was higher,

the downtown was more lovely, and

the streets were cleaner.

But my heart, which was catching up from the move, was echoing Moses's encounter: "My presence will go with you, and I will give you rest." And I was giving God every reason to move His presence to an easier place, but that wasn't going to happen. It was time to start thinking differently—to start looking at what I already had in me, then start to imagine all that God wanted to do through me.

First Thirty-One Days

I needed a plan if I was going to start to stay—and it needed to fit my personality. First, I had to unpack every single box. Nothing says "stay" until the cardboard is destroyed—or at least broken down and stored under beds.

I was old enough to know what I liked, and would figure out how to do those things here. I knew I could do parks. I enjoyed local events. I loved prepared-in-advance adventures. So, naturally, I drew up a plan for our family that I called "Thirty-One Days in the City" as a way to get out of the house and get to know the people and places. We would learn new things. We would attempt hard things. And we would make a list of what worked and what didn't work, what we enjoyed and what we were okay never doing again! Since it was summer and the kids were not in school, we did something every day for those first thirty-one days. We got library cards, visited with the elderly at the assisted living home across the street, enjoyed a free day at the zoo, and asked friends back home to write so we could get real mail.

Abraham's First Thirty-One Days

Mine and Abraham's first days looked slightly different from one another. He traveled with a zoo, was elderly himself, and would be featured in a bestseller one day. Yet, similarly, our families saw the difficulties to come and went anyway. We saw God and said yes. We couldn't, and still can't, see all God has in store, but Abraham's story and example helps us. Thanks, God, for that bestseller!

> The LORD said to Abram, after Lot had separated from him. . . . "Arise, walk through the length and the breadth of the land, for I will give it to you." So Abram moved his tent and came and settled by the oaks of Mamre, which are at Hebron, and there he built an altar to the LORD. (Gen. 13:14, 17–18)

It reads poetically simple and clear, but the next chapter tells of all the leaders at war in the land. God told Abraham to look around in all directions. God did this once Abraham was alone. I like that God shows us things when no one else is around—just you and Him. Anyway, Lot had already gone to his pretty piece of land, which, ironically, was Sodom. I believe that Abraham was able to see what God saw in that moment perhaps because he was already in a faith-filled season of moving his family. Let's consider the action steps Abraham took as he started to stay:

Arise
Walk
Settle
Build

Arise

Abraham had to leave familiar and family, but he gained peace and perspective. For us, we knew who lived in San Francisco. We also knew who didn't live here—primarily our parents and siblings. When we are separated from comfort, friends, and family, we are not separated from God. God abundantly makes up for anything we could consider loss.

That's why we have to do what God told the Israelites to do later on: "Stop the murmuring in the tents!" The Israelites said that the Lord hated them (Deut. 1:27). They measured themselves to those around them, who were greater and taller. They felt small compared to the cities that were "great and fortified up to heaven" (v. 28).

Paralysis will set in if we over-deliberate and avoid making decisions. When we freeze up in fear, we crawl back into the very moving boxes that got us here. It's just impossible for us to seal the boxes from the outside while we're crouched down on the inside. Ben and I faced many fears in our being sent, but the towering and triumphant fear was this: What if we don't go for it? What if we fear the risk rather than follow the God of possibilities?

Remember the faithfulness of God, abandon the fear of man, fight the urge to flee, and start to stay.

Walk

God had Abraham walk through the land to see it more clearly. If God was giving him the land, this only makes sense. When we see that no matter where we live we are still within the kingdom of God, the moves don't become the dominant factor. What matters is how we are going to invest and contribute and live like we're supposed to be there.

We have the privilege of getting to know the land. We set our feet upon the places He has for us. Even if we didn't think we'd live in San Francisco forever, we chose to start to stay for now.

I needed to walk forward and not be one of "those who shrink back and are destroyed, but of those who have faith and preserve their souls" (Heb. 10:39). Ben and I started to think about what it could look like to be part of a group of people who made a significant commitment to live with purpose in San Francisco. When we start to think, we start to dream. When we start to dream, we tap into the supernatural, which can only be achieved with the hand of God.

What if we started to think *I can stay here* rather than *I've got to get out of here*? What if we could become family for each other—not to replace our physical families, who may live far away, but to share such dynamic community that *family* seems the only appropriate word to describe what we have together? What if we used our short time on earth to invest in a place for eternity? These thoughts will come as we walk the places we call home. *What if?*

Settle

Abraham moved his tent and came and settled. Moved? Check. Came and settled? Uh. No. You have been calling this place "home" for months, maybe even years, but you haven't started to *stay* yet. There's still that one last box that needs to be unpacked. You've been hoping for a move, a job transfer, a change of address, a sunnier day, or a bus to come by and pick you up, but God has you right where He wants you. So start to stay.

If you keep thinking about your next move or how many more months you have to live here, you won't settle in, plug in, get involved, or make a difference. You won't really care. You will only consume and not contribute. You will be an expense to the community rather than an asset.

To settle means to dwell. To pitch our tent as Abraham did, we have to envision ourselves in our location. Ask yourself, *What's attractive? What do I love about where I live? What has me here in the first place?* Most of us don't live in the neighborhood of "love at first sight" anyway. Invite us over if you do.

This is more of a mental, internal affair than blasting to your city block or subdivision, "Hey, we're here and we're thinking about sticking around." This mentality and decision are because you know God has you here, and you're aware that reality is bigger than anything Target or Crate and Barrel can offer. Society can help us set up home and make it sparkle, but not even REI can sell tents that come with this kind of package.

I had to tell myself to stop sulking and start staying. A perfect place doesn't exist on this side of heaven. We will only experience that city when our time on earth is done.

Besides, longevity is attractive. It's the best product on the market that's foundational and stable. Take it from the San Francisco sea lions. They used to live on Seal Rock in the bay. After the 1989 earthquake, they moved to Pier 39.[2] Fishermen couldn't get to their boats and had to get the city involved. City workers and mariners sprayed them, but the seals loved the water massages and decided to stay. They're now the top tourist attraction in the city.

That's what longevity and determination get us! What are you doing for the long haul? How can dwellers of faith be an attractive piece of the town where you live?

When we choose to settle in and determine not to leave when it's hard, we're ready to build the altar.

Build

At this time Abraham built an altar. It was his third. (Gen. 12:7–8). Everywhere he moved, he built one as a symbolic way of giving thanks to God.

Abraham pitched his tent and built an altar and called upon the name of the Lord even though the Canaanites were in the land. Even though Lot chose the prettier land. Even though war was looming nearby. Even though there were more unknowns than knowns.

You've called this place home for some time. Have you given thanks to God for bringing you here? Keeping you here? Calling you here? We should never take our land for granted.

We've built altars in each of our homes in a few different ways. We give our home a name that is symbolic of how God has provided or moved. Our home is called "the dwelling place." We choose a Scripture that declares a promise or truth that we want present in every room of our house. These are written on post-it notes hung in discreet places. In every home we've lived, we've given each part of it to God.

This helps with settling. This helps us stay. We stay because it's right, because God has a plan, because our gifts are to be used here, because God cares for this people, because He hasn't told us to go anywhere else. Let's stop looking to leave and start to stay.

DWELLER TIP

It's okay for others to see where you live—your mess, how your kids behave at home—without feeling the need to strive for perfection. I'm learning that being vulnerable with my space makes me feel more connected and more real.

—Anna, recovering perfectionist

welcome mat

• • • • • •

But seek the welfare of the city where I have sent you into exile, and pray to the LORD on its behalf, for in its welfare you will find your welfare.

Jeremiah 29:7

5

Jesus Is Here

The city might have been new to me but not to Jesus. He was already here. I'd believed in Him all my life. My head was packed with spiritual knowledge, but in the town of six traffic lights, the Midwest, and the places in between, I rarely got the opportunity to put my spiritual knowledge to use outside of my operational Christian culture. This was my fault. I preferred comfort zones and white picket fences. I didn't have those where I lived now.

One autumn afternoon, the kids and I were at the park for soccer practice. I spread out a blanket and invited another soccer mom to come and sit if she wanted. We were familiar with each other since we had children at the same school and on the same team.

We entered into conversation about the Indian summer weather and her pregnancy. She turned the question to our motivation for moving to the city. My palms always produce a substantial amount of sweat in these moments.

"So what brought you to the city?" she asked.

Unjamming the words in my throat, I said, "To start a church."

"Oh, what kind of church?"

"A Christian church."

I explained as broadly as I could that we had moved to start a church from scratch. We didn't talk denominations, as that wouldn't translate. A church that didn't have a building yet but had a staff that had also relocated from the other side of the country. A church that was for all people but had no people yet. I was beginning to wonder again why we had moved. I went on to answer her questions as she wondered out loud what we believed. Yes, my husband teaches. He uses the Bible. The messages are relevant and applicable for daily living. No, we have a band with a guitar and drums.

"What do you believe in that you would move here to start a church?"

Awkward pause.

Shauna, don't mess up, here. You haven't been in many conversations that draw out such answers.

"God, our Father and Creator, sent His perfect Son, Jesus, to show us how to live and serve and love. His Son ultimately died on the cross for all of our wrongs and then was raised back to life so that we might have eternal hope and eternal life. We center our lives around these truths and His teachings in the Bible."

I only wish my answer was that eloquent.

"Well, um . . ." Stumble. Scratch head. "We believe in God the Father, Jesus the Son, and the Holy Spirit."

"I've heard of God, but who's this Jesus you're talking about?" she asked.

Wake up, Shauna. She's asking you a question, I told myself. My brain rattled. Its wheels were squeaky.

How was it that I was looking at her the same way she was looking at me? We both needed to know *who* Jesus was. As I looked around, I also needed to know *where* He was.

It's foggy, but I think I managed to stumble over the truths that Jesus is God's only Son, who lived here on earth so that we can have forgiveness of our sins and a relationship with God the Father.

One of my boys was close enough to hear the conversation. His smile came from heaven. He saw his bashful mom fumble but refuse to fail. He saw me strive for a new friendship despite how different our lives might be. It's not like I was explaining software engineering in French. I was telling her what we do and what we believe. In English.

That initial conversation has been foundational and instrumental over the past few years. I've learned more about my friend's Iranian heritage and have prayed with her as her brother battled cancer. She is gracious to me for the countless times I have invited her to our church. And this school mom-friend returns such grace in keeping an extra eye on the kids on the playground after school.

That field was prepared because God was already ahead of me, knowing this would take place. I was awakened to Jesus in a powerful way. I had found Jesus on a soccer field in the Castro district. And if He was here, like I believed, I didn't want to be anywhere else. Not that He was hiding. It's just that He was in places I was finding myself in—and these places weren't church buildings or religious gatherings. I could stay because Jesus was here. And that started to matter more than anything else that had comforted me in the past.

It would be a career woman, some techies, a World Series celebration, the smell of urine, and a city view that would prove these discoveries true again. I saw my self-absorbed approach—and then I saw what happened when I started looking for Jesus.

Career Woman

She reached out to take a granola bar and an invite card from a member of one of our mission teams who was helping us launch the church. It turned out to be much more than a simple gesture. She was just coming out of a depressive stretch as a new mom, working woman, and youngster in her faith. Her name was Anna, and she started coming to our launch team meetings in our apartment. Friendship formed immediately because of our connection as believers. While we were so delighted to have another warm soul join our team (self-absorbed), we were more ecstatic that we had a new friend (looking for Jesus).

Some Techies

I pushed my three boys in a stroller built for two up to a nearby park. I was determined to get out and about and remind them what playground equipment was like. At high noon on a weekday, I was surprised to see the wooden structure so crowded. Every swing was occupied. The slide was stacked. Toes were in the sandbox. But everyone was a twentysomething techie eating their foil-wrapped burritos. If I was self-absorbed, these techies were on my kids' new playground. But if I saw Jesus here, these techies were sharing ideas during a much-needed break in a different setting so they could go and change the world. I motioned for the boys to run around them and with them. Maybe they would change the world together.

World Series Celebration

Nighttime came and we weren't staying inside. The celebration was right outside our doors. Police had streets barricaded, but other than that, anything was allowed. The Giants had just won the World Series and people cascaded out of their homes onto the streets to give high fives and toast with their drinks. It was a police officer who pointed out that our city rebels when bound. If I was self-absorbed, this town was disturbing our peace and should celebrate in a more civilized manner. But if I was looking for Jesus, our city knew how to celebrate and party better without restrictions. We would give our high fives freely!

The Smell of Urine

The smell of urine captivated my senses as I got off the train at my stop. Bright fluorescent lighting doesn't keep thirty or so people from sleeping here, all sprawled out. My self-absorption tells me they don't belong here and are in my way. They are a nuisance and a contamination. But if I change lenses, I see individuals who are hurting and need a place to lay their heads. I see a brother, father, sister, and aunt. I make sure to say the same hello to them as I would to the businessperson. For we are all of the same Father.

The City View

There's a place I like to go to see the city view, up on a hill, where I can see a heart shape cut out. My selfish view is of an expensive city that presents challenges for raising a family and living out my faith. But then I see Jesus looking at the same view with me. I realize His love is much bigger than the little I can express. His heart is for the people of this place.

. . . . . .

I was learning: He's already here. I found Him in the train station, at the park, and on the streets. Anna found Jesus in a community that formed through a granola bar and an invite card. Julia, the president of a large civic organization, saw Jesus at parades and city meetings, and Brett, a volunteer at our church, saw Him at company headquarters. He's right here. Around the corner. In others. Ahead of us. This is our greatest comfort where we live. This is our motivation to stay. It's our reason to pack up and move to where Jesus is leading us. We pick up where others have left off. We join others in finding Jesus throughout the community.

None of us are the first faith dwellers in our towns. We aren't going to be the last ones either. Before our move, we met other faith dwellers in the city—beautiful remnants holding tight to Christ and refusing to give up or give in. They had started to stay years ago. They had prayed and planted seeds before we got to San Francisco. One was serving in a homeless shelter in the

Haight-Ashbury district. Another was strategizing to help church communities thrive. A family moved to be tentmakers and public school advocates and love their neighborhood well. Jesus was inside His people inside our city gates and not confined to where I thought He would be.

I had a poetic thought:

> If our city had a gate and I knew Jesus was about to come in,
> I'd be there to greet Him, to welcome Him in.
> I'd thank Him for coming,
> shower Him with praise—
> stating the obvious to the Ancient of Days.
> I'd tell Jesus that I know He heals, comforts and mourns.
> That He sits with the outcasts, breaks the chains of sin
>   and bondage, sets us free, and loves everyone.
> I'd show Him the beautiful places—all of which He made—
> the bay, the hills, the cliffs on His ocean's edge.
> The lavender, succulents, and calla lilies that grow wild.
> The seals, the canyons, the overflowing fruit outside the
>   markets, the tide.
> I'd want Him to see what His people were doing—
> serving in the hard places, painting nails, caring for their
>   little ones, delivering meals, reading to children, work-
>   ing with integrity, starting companies that make a
>   difference—and He'd know all that already.
> I would still want to show Him believers meeting in small
>   groups at churches, in homes, in coffee shops and
>   playgrounds—speaking encouragement, holding one
>   another up, celebrating, mourning, and every day living
>   in community.
> Starting conversations on the bus, giving smiles away,
>   listening to coworkers, collaborating to bring about
>   good change to His world, inviting others in, building
>   relationships.
> I'd want to show Him the hard places—
> places that need His power at work and His kingdom come.

Places like our schools, our government buildings, apartments where the lonely hide, and streets where the homeless abide.

The neighborhoods and alleyways where people fight for their rights without considering the rights He gave up for us all.

Where tolerance is expected without consideration of the cross.

We'd finish up at my house over a cup of water, coffee, or tea.

I'd certainly offer Him all three.

My heart would be heavy, and I'd start my confession— that I see and don't respond. Fear and don't believe.

That I keep busy in my self-absorption and don't always walk in His purpose for me.

And I'd imagine He would do what He does for every other soul He has tended . . .

He would be gentle and kind and speak His very words of wisdom.

I would drink in His forgiveness and His grace and rise up, because, really, I'd just been in His presence and He in my place.

And as He left, I wouldn't hesitate to stand at the door to my house and keep the door open.

Keep calling Him in.

Keep needing Him more.

Keep loving my own, the lost, the poor.

For He is always welcome here, and I will choose today to live like it more than ever before.

I get your fears and worries, though. I like "nearness" with flesh on. Someone else to be with me, who shares commonalities and values. Strength is found in numbers. And though we agreed to follow God to San Francisco even if it meant it was just the five of us, I was relieved to know nine others were moving with us. God doesn't guarantee flesh, but He always promises Himself.

"Nevertheless, I am continually with you; you hold my right hand. You guide me with your counsel . . . it is good to be near God; I have made the Lord GOD my refuge, that I may tell of all your works" (Ps. 73:23–24, 28). May God give you an experience that requires you to need His presence more than anything else.

He wants to come inside your place as much as He wants you to see Him outside. Stand on the welcome mat of your door. You don't have to look far. You might be in the minority. Speak another language. Be the only one of your kind in your neighborhood. Only have a green card. You are welcome here. You have value and purpose in this place. If that welcome mat is for no other purpose, let it remind you that, each time you step inside or outside your dwelling, you are empowered with this truth: He welcomes you. That is well worth it. "Behold, I stand at the door and knock. If anyone hears my voice and opens the door, I will come in to him and eat with him, and he with me" (Rev. 3:20). For when you feel welcomed, you'll want to make others feel welcomed too.

Look around you. Jesus is nearby. Seriously, look around. Where is He sitting? Or is He standing? He's at the foot of the bed. He's right beside you. Can't see Him? Look for the effects that indicate He is by you. For He has a purpose and a plan and is carrying it out. It's time for us to join Him in it.

DWELLER TIP

Ask the customer about her day. Learn her name. She just might serve the same God.

—Israel, barista

6

God's Plan for Places

I couldn't find that hidden park smothered in eucalyptus if I tried.
I do remember mansions on hills and a sweeping view of the bay.
The sky was blue. A jacket was needed. I can find the picture
of that moment though. It's framed against our initial city map,
where we marked in black pen the boundaries where we'd start
the church. I can also recall the verse we prayed then: Jeremiah
29:7. "But seek the welfare of the city where I have sent you into
exile, and pray to the LORD on its behalf, for in its welfare you
will find your welfare."

And the verse we claimed for the place we would now live is
Jeremiah 33:9.

> And this city shall be to me a name of joy, a praise and a glory
> before all the nations of the earth who shall hear of all the good
> that I do for them. They shall fear and tremble because of all the
> good and all the prosperity I provide for it.

I could lay eyes on the land God was giving us. And it's a good
thing I could pray the Scriptures, because my soul prayer sounded
more like, "Are You sure, God?" His plan is to give us the land, and

for us to take it for future generations. Physical location matters to His plan, be it Babylon or Beijing or Boston.

God Gives Us the Land . . .

Moses had the hard task of leading two or three million Israelites into a land among "seven nations more numerous and mightier" than themselves (Deut. 7:1). Still, God let them know that the land was His (Lev. 25:23). As the people multiplied, Moses challenged them to appoint wise leaders to oversee the God-given land. "See, the LORD your God has set the land before you. Go up, take possession, as the LORD, the God of your fathers, has told you. Do not fear or be dismayed" (Deut. 1:21). God wants us to see the land that He has given us as His. It's being managed by mayors, judges, and government officials. It's being prayed for by us. It has dark places and broken places. He knows that. What we need to know is that the land is His, and we must claim it for Him and not feel as if we are trespassing. No matter the number of people per square mile in your neck of the woods, 100 percent aren't living kingdom-minded.

This changes the way we look at those on the sidewalk as we pass by. We share this land. The property our home is on is His. The rough part of town is His. So is the new, attractive part. He's been in the habit of giving His land to His people. He is kind to walk among us, be our God, and let us be His people (Lev. 26:12). He does this so that we take it for future generations.

. . . So That We Take It for Future Generations

"See, I have set the land before you. Go in and take possession of the land that the LORD swore to your fathers, to Abraham, to Isaac, and to Jacob, to give to them and to their offspring after them" (Deut. 1:8). Joshua and Caleb were the only two spies out of the twelve who returned and believed they could take the land God was giving them. It would be Caleb, decades later, who would be gifted that very piece of land because of his faithfulness.

For us, others prayed, watered, and sowed before we got here. They did this for us. Now we get to take care of this place for those who will come after us. What we do in our land is what the next generation will inherit. What is seen and unseen. What we build, shape, and create will be what others step into.

While we live in the land with the future in mind, God wants us to leave footprints, plant gardens, and learn the culture. This is our gift to those who come after us.

Leave Footprints (Watch for Wonders)

God doesn't always leave footprints, but He wants us to. Let's stand in the Red Sea, the ground mushy beneath our feet. Massive aquariums are to our left and right. Rapid heart palpitations are to be expected. With the enemy just behind, the millions of no-longer-slaves look ahead to their brother leaders, Moses and Aaron.

Psalm 77 points out the signs and wonders from God—His power and presence cannot be denied and He confirms they are where they are supposed to be. But it's one verse that grips me. "Your way was through the sea, your path through the great waters; yet your footprints were unseen. You led your people like a flock by the hand of Moses and Aaron" (Ps. 77:19–20). His command. Our obedience. His signs and wonders, miracles and provision. Moses and Aaron at the front to lead the people through a water He had created and then parted for this moment in history.

His unseen footprints lead to our faith being exercised. He'll come through. Always. It's just that we might not always see evidence of it. Herein lies the key to God's plan for places.

Where God is leading is often unseen. He chooses to use people who will walk by faith, as Moses and Aaron experienced. We've experienced it too, as we couldn't see His footprints at the time but look back and see those who have followed us here, who are also leaving footprints themselves. We are creatures with a propensity toward what is seen. I'd prefer to hike a well-worn trail. I'm a fan of clear directions in the airport. Line starts here. Groups 1, 2, 3, and 4. West Maroon Creek Trail this way. Yet wonders happen in the unseen.

So, whose footprints are there? Yours. Mine. Moses's and Aaron's. Our family's personal footprints have led to Eddie and Sarah, Jason and Jen, James and Desiree. To John and Jennifer. To the Takemoto family. To our kindergarten teacher sponsoring a child through Compassion International. To a school family giving church a try for the first time. To Rekha the nurse. The psalmist prays, "Make me to know your ways . . . lead me in your truth" (Psalm 25:4–5). But anything about footprints? Nope. Just Psalm 77. God shows us the path. He says, "That is the way; walk in it." He positions people, young and old, novice and experienced. Then He expects us to leave footprints. This is it—walking into and through the land He has for us. Awakening to love where you live. Unseen footprints lead us to watch for His wonders.

Plant Gardens

Have you lived in your current place longer than you intended or thought you would? My hand is in the air! We are exiles because we are not home yet. Put yourself among the barley fields of Babylon. It's the exiles, the Israelites, who planted and tended these. They were not gluttons for punishment. They were forced there. God had a plan for them in Babylon, the place where He sent them. Jeremiah 29:4 is addressed "To all the exiles whom I have sent." He is the Sending God.

God gave them ideas of what He intended for them to do while living in a place where they were exiles. What we do where we live benefits the land and the people. What goes into the earth brings forth bounty that is to be enjoyed by all. I have a garden at Costco, multiple schools, a sports field, our neighborhood, and the gym.

Where are your gardens? Tend them. They are on the land He has given us. God might not have us building houses but renting or buying. Planting gardens might look like buying local produce. We are to use our gifts and talents to help cure, develop, teach, build, uncover, expand, multiply, and give to our corners of the world, which God can take and use for His good.

Learn the Culture

Imagine Paul standing up in the city hub in Athens, Greece. He doesn't walk onto the scene as the new kid on the block with a briefcase filled with his ideas of what to do with the city. Rather, he only spoke after he learned the people and the culture. After he got himself established in the town. He spoke as a concerned citizen, not as a curious Christian. He walked around and observed the culture and the people. He could tell they all had something they treasured most, and the people couldn't see what they were missing. That's why, after Paul became a learner of the culture, he earned the favor to stand and speak to fellow dwellers.

> The God who made the world and everything in it, being Lord of heaven and earth, does not live in temples made by man, nor is he served by human hands, as though he needed anything, since he himself gives to all mankind life and breath and everything. And he made from one man every nation of mankind to live on all the face of the earth, having determined allotted periods and the boundaries of their dwelling place, that they should seek God, and perhaps feel their way toward him and find him. (Acts 17:24–27)

This is our story of His plan. God made us, the whole world, and everything in it. He decides where we live, work, play, and sleep so that we will seek Him and indeed find Him. He loves us this much. He loves our neighbors and our coworkers this much! We get to declare and they get to respond. We share our story in hopes they will want more. Our stories can include the big picture and the daily parts of life. Let them in on the highs, lows, struggles, and joys.

This is our part of His plan. We must declare! We must proclaim! We must tell our story with Jesus as the main character and tell how He's placed us where we live. We tell it in ongoing conversations on the train, in the copy room, at the gym. In the shared parking garage, at the farmer's market, and around the table.

We learn about the people who live in our community, what they celebrate and how they grieve. Where they moved from and what their childhoods were like. We pay attention for commonalities and moments to introduce Jesus.

We initially see our new place as having potential for change and we desire to fall in love with it. If this vision fades it's because we've relied on ourselves to bring about the change and grow our appreciation. Rather, we accept His invitation to love a culture, a people group, like He does, using the creativity He has graciously given us. See the place you live and walk its streets. See God in your day. Get creative with His command to live sent. Go, be, do, say, pray. He sees the people. He knows our potential.

In my city, I've got a lifetime of people to love. The immigrants. The refugees. The under-resourced. The minorities. They sit beside me at church and are on our sports teams. They lead us in worship, in business decisions, in community and technology, and in science and education. They are our next-door neighbors. They love. They help. They teach. They are a part of the kingdom of God, and I joyfully say, "You are welcomed here." Learn the culture that God loves more than we do.

· · · · · ·

Come up the hill with me to Walter Haas park. We'll get a city view rather than a street view. Follow me over to the bench near the edge of the cliff. Don't look down, just up and out. The air is more fresh and the mind less cluttered. We're above the hustle and bustle, and the tight quarters below can't be felt anymore. It's at this park that I've heard Jesus say, *Follow Me. It's My mission. My plan. You don't have to create it, but I want you to creatively live it out. It's not your agenda people need to rally around. It's Me. Only Me.*

Jesus is here, He's got a plan, and we step into what He's already started and join those who have gone before us to see His plan fulfilled in the places we call home. He's forward thinking, always ahead of all things, above all things, in all things.

Look up. Do you see the heart shape of the city as it bends to a point at the skyscrapers? The love for where you live matters on days when His plan is questioned.

All of Scripture speaks to the importance of place. From God putting Adam and Eve in the Garden of Eden to Joseph journeying to Egypt to Daniel being captive in the land of Babylon to the exact location where you are living today.

DWELLER TIP

We are truly blessed by the family God has given us and we feel the call to open the doors of our home to some little ones in need in our community, and also connect with their families and pour some much-needed love in their lives.

—The Moas, foster family

7

The Enemy Has a Plan Too

The devil doesn't like us loving where we live, so clearly he's going to either paint the town bleak and black or distract us with glitz and glamour. And in my household the devil particularly messes with us on Saturday nights.

It became standard to prop open our bedroom windows in the evening after the sun had come with force during the day. We'd be prepared for the next day, but without fail, Ben would ask, "Is anyone going to show up at church tomorrow?" If I could have spoken out of both sides of my mouth at the same time, I'd have said to my pastor husband, "Of course they will!" and at the same time begged Jesus, "Please, Jesus, please."

The other standard part was the "swarms of bugs" we'd fight off during the night. All in our sleep. I'd think I was the only one under attack and would beg for God's nearness. Just after Jesus had lulled me back to sleep, Ben would wake minutes later to call on God to speak truth and surround our home. We'd wake on Sunday morning and to our surprise have no bug bites. This made sense, because there are few flying bugs in the city, yet we'd stare at each other knowing what we had felt throughout the night. We had done battle with the one who wasn't happy it was Sunday morning. There were no bugs, only battles. And these battles were fiercest during the weeks when we'd have people over to our apartment and fill our living space with dozens of people for launch team meetings as we figured out how to do community and build a church.

I chanted Hezekiah's prayer in 2 Kings 19:19 every Friday night, because Saturday and Sunday always followed: "So now, O LORD our God, save us, please, from his hand, that all the kingdoms of the earth may know that you, O LORD, are God alone." It was becoming increasingly clear that while God was giving us the land, we were encroaching on someone else's territory. And the enemy of God, Satan, wasn't letting us forget about it.

His Tactics

Brokenness was all around us. Daily. I want you to meet Hannah. Our family called her "Homeless Hannah," with respect. She lived in our neighborhood, perused the grocery aisles, and came into the bank and pharmacy. Some days she was in her right mind to converse with, so we'd say hello. Hannah was drawn to the boys because they reminded her of her happy childhood, as she was one of nine kids. But otherwise Hannah was not approachable. We often saw her wandering the streets near the post office, the bank, and the train station. I learned her story on sane days and cried out to God on the other days. Our hearts hurt for Hannah. She was a high priority on the family bedtime prayer list.

One day Ben and Elijah were picking up a snack at the store and a man outside was asking for money. Ben handed him a dollar and asked the man what he intended to do with the money. The man bent down and made intentional eye contact with Elijah. "Kid, don't ever get into drugs. You'll be like me." He turned to Ben. "Honestly, sir, I need drugs." Brokenness.

Soon after, our kids stepped outside our apartment so I could spray their hair for crazy hair day. I was following when I heard, "Hey, Mom, there's a man asleep out here." I waved my arms frantically since my feet weren't moving fast enough. They got the idea and came back inside.

Where in the world do we live? was the thought on repeat in my head. As we investigated, we determined that this homeless man had slept closer to our son that night on the lower level than we did two floors above. Brokenness. This isn't the way the world should be. This isn't the way my city should be.

The situations seemed hopeless. That's right where the enemy wants us all. For faith dwellers to feel scared, secluded, superior. Scared of our surroundings. Secluded from community. Superior to the people around us. For others to feel depressed, discouraged, and in the dark. Do you see how he divides? His plan is to keep citizens on two different sides of the tracks. He's the one who is responsible for the "me/them" mentality. It's all his doing. He's got us separated. Us afraid to go to them. Them enjoying the dark while we selfishly lavish the light only upon ourselves. Like it's ours to begin with, anyway. Just another one of his dirty schemes.

To be quite frank, it's not the religious the enemy has an interest in. He smiles at the churches who worship tradition and rule themselves. It's the Christians believing God with big faith and going out in the community among the people He's called them to reach. This is when he puts on his lion costume—it's never cute and always deadly. Because someone is going down.

To Keep Others in the Dark and Discouraged

October is a month of darkness where I live. It's taken me a few autumn seasons to realize the pattern. I saw a businesswoman dancing provocatively in her pencil skirt and satin blouse. She did so in an open area while other businesspeople ate outdoors. She began to remove some clothing.

A clean shaven man in dress pants and a valet parking jacket was staggering drunk in front of the transit station, blocking the entrance.

A barely dressed person was escorted out of a store in front of me as three teenagers made fun of the situation by posting on social media. Later, I saw this person being arrested in front of another nearby store. And this all happened in a few hours, between my birthday lunch with Ben and school pick-up.

We must recognize our battle is not with the people of the city but the deceiver of the city. Tentmaker Paul told the dwellers in Ephesus that our battle isn't against flesh and blood but against the powers of darkness, against the devil, against the spiritual forces of evil in the heavenly places (Eph. 6:12).

I should have seen it coming. Tuesday was quite eventful for our family, small group, and church. My heart was hurting for a struggling marriage. A young student at school was unclear about her gender. An assembly was scheduled at school later this week where altars would be presented and prayers would be offered up for the dead.

Instead, I was focused on laundry, cleaning, school lunches, and bedtime. I crashed, exhausted, at 10:30. During pockets of time between three and four in the morning, my soul wrestled. My mind ran. I tossed and turned with anxiety aching my body. The younger two kids awoke. I snapped at them to return to bed. My mouth was dry. I was dehydrated, for Tuesday literally emptied me of all that quenches thirst.

With little energy and weary eyes, my soul cried *Jesus. Jesus. Jesus.* I begged for His army of angels to encamp around us. I begged for all evil, demonic forces to be purged from our home. I was desperate for His nearness.

There was a spiritual battle going on to keep us distracted and discouraged. Our family name was mentioned again in the heavenlies—the Pilgreens. It's good to have your name mentioned in battle. Spoken, shouted, or whispered. It's as if I heard Jesus say, *Shauna, daughter, you and your family are worth fighting for.*

The enemy definitely has a plan against a people, a family, a church, a remnant, a place that is seeking God. No shocker there. We can take off our surprised face. When opposition is felt, pay attention. Take inventory:

Is this fear? If so, what's making me afraid?

Am I doing or thinking something I know is wrong? Confess it.

Does someone quickly come to mind who unsettles my nerves? Make it right with them—even by sending a text to encourage or to set up a time to meet.

What is on my calendar? Something the enemy doesn't like?

When you've said yes to staying and living sent, the enemy will unleash his tactics to keep you scared, secluded, and superior.

To Keep Us Scared, Secluded, and Superior

They didn't care who we were or that we were new or that I had three littles with me or that I had fed the meter or that I really wanted to love this place. I was in their spot and was going to pay for it. It pains me to write such an unexpected adventure. I'm still not laughing about it, and if you knew how much we had to pay, you'd stop the chuckling pretty fast. Only the guy towing away our van has permission to laugh and shake his head. And preferably when I'm not looking!

The short of it is that we wanted to take Aunt Lindsey to Chinatown and didn't have much time. And instead of paying the price for public transit, we opted for the cheaper route of meter parking on the street. I did notice a public parking garage that charged $7.50 per hour, but knew we could do better than that. So we settled in between two cars on the street and filled the meter with $3.50 in coins to give us one glorious hour of parking.

Now, I'd lived in the city long enough to know that you read the signs around you and remember the cross streets of where you parked. So I noticed Grant and Sutter Streets and that I only had one hour. I also noticed the signs on the street posts that said the times and days for street cleaning and knew we were good there.

What I didn't notice were the stickers down the post of the meter that said "commercial loading zone," and included a phone number hotline in case your car is towed. So we looked closely at our watches and then enjoyed the next fifty-four minutes in Chinatown!

To my regurgitating stomach and shocked eyes, the van was *not* where we left it! I knew it had been either towed or stolen, and after I read the fine print on the meter pole, I knew the outcome. Fear took over in such an oppressive manner. Much had to do with the three little hands I was holding. The city grew dark in the moment, and I grew small.

In a matter of a few hours, Ben had retrieved our van from the Auto Return Yard and paid the hefty fine. We took public transit back home and I locked the apartment door.

. . . . . .

After the incident, I wasn't driving much and getting to the restaurant would be a beautiful walk along the Embarcadero. We set out to celebrate a friend getting a job after months of searching. I know that city planning didn't make San Francisco sidewalks with children in mind, but our three boys scooted and ran like it anyway. We called them closer as we saw several bikes coming up ahead and didn't want any collisions. As the bikes got closer to us, we became certain of a shocking reality. These men had nothing on. Nothing at all. Elijah reached up as high as he could to cover his momma's eyes. It was moments before the shock wore off. To be quite honest, it hasn't, really. While the shock jolts us, it leaves a residue of anxiety and apprehension.

The enemy wants us to make our earthly pursuits our top goal. This is an easy tactic, considering the time, money, and energy we give them. If the enemy can get us slightly distracted, slightly off course, he's succeeding. John Ortberg, a Bay Area dweller and pastor, refers to this as a shadow mission—a little off course is just enough to shift our focus and step away from God's best.

When We Are Pursuing God, the Enemy Will Pursue Us

I have written this book as a witness to how we're living this way in a particularly broken place so that more people can dwell strategically and purposefully, hear God's voice, know where to walk, and recognize other voices and distractions. We ask God to bless the land, give us favor, lead the way, and fight for us and with us.

For if God has a plan for where we live, then the Deceiver is working against dwellers of faith to make us feel isolated and secluded. He megaphones voices that distract us from the truth. It's not a onetime thing either. Basically, get used to it!

And at the same time, take heart. Peter is referred to as the apostle of hope. These words of his are heavy but hopeful:

> Be sober-minded; be watchful. Your adversary the devil prowls around like a roaring lion, seeking someone to devour. Resist him, firm in your faith, knowing that the same kinds of suffering are being experienced by your brotherhood throughout the world. And after you have suffered a little while, the God of all grace, who has called you to his eternal glory in Christ, will himself restore, confirm, strengthen, and establish you. To him be the dominion forever and ever. Amen. (1 Pet. 5:8–11)

If we don't live this way, we give the enemy our land, our community. We invite apathy in whether we technically ordered it or not. Oh, but the enemy did! Satan wants us to avoid these action steps in 1 Peter 5 and stay on the sidelines, leaving people in the dark. But Jesus gave us the gift of salvation, not so that we would kick up our feet on the rescue raft but rather serve Him and love others without fear and with purpose. Therein lies the victory.

We have to change the way we are living. We need His plan, His Spirit, His direction, His shelter, His protection. We can see how things went terribly bad when the Israelites carried out a plan that wasn't His. They made a formation that left out the Spirit. They moved into Egypt without God's direction. They sought refuge from a powerful head. God turned the place and power into shame and humiliation for the people (Isa. 30:1–3).

Often we wonder where God is leading and *if* He's leading. At times, He's fighting for us from behind. We must keep looking forward and let God fight our battles as we go in and take the land. Remember that His footprints were unseen through the Red Sea. Where was God? He was behind them, fighting the Egyptians and showing off His glory!

We must recognize His voice that comes from behind as we take those steps of faith forward. And when we do, it scatters those distractions and the glitz and glamour of comfort and ease. "Be gone," is what we say. "Be gone! The enemy will not win my city!"

He's looking for the dwellers living sent. We're targets. Stay in the world. That's how to battle it out. Unfortunately, the Christian culture amid the American church has proclaimed that we have to be removed from it all or else we'll be seen to be "like them," and that would be a terrible idea. Pursuing God takes us into the heart of our culture and community. Be found faithful where He's at work.

Proclaiming Jesus will lead to pushback. Not experiencing pushback? One of two things is happening. You are only surrounded by people who think like you. Or you aren't having conversations about Christ.

We get to engage with Almighty God to see His kingdom come to our towns and cities. God responds to our faith, our communing with Him. In the Gospel of John, Jesus didn't want His disciples removed from the world but rather protected from the evil one, knowing that if they stayed and engaged they'd definitely need the protection. Jesus offered a prayer, not for worldly protection but spiritual protection.

"[God] has delivered us from the domain of darkness and transferred us to the kingdom of his beloved Son" (Col. 1:13). That's the wonder of place. None of us have to live in darkness. We can live in the light, and whosoever chooses to may as well. Just because the enemy has a plan doesn't mean we have to flesh it out for him.

Our enemy can't see the future, only the past and the present. So he uses fear. We fire back with hope, because we *know* the future. That's a weapon he doesn't have! And he'll use packaging tape and bubble wrap to secure fear all over us, keeping us isolated, when we're meant to live sent together. To cross the street. To meet the neighbors. Because it's no longer you and me and them. It's profoundly *us*.

DWELLER TIP

For the sake of our marriage and theirs, we double date often with many couples who are almost young enough to be our own kids.

—Bill and Rhonda Poppen, empty nesters

8

Meet the Neighbors

Wouldn't it be great to have a welcome committee in each and every town? The moving van rolls in, tambourines sound, and a marching band escorts you down Main Street. The committee shows up at your front door, applauding to have someone new in town. They shower you with pantry items and fresh flowers for the table. The service companies arrive shortly to turn everything on for you. Just as you sit down to rest your feet and wonder what's for dinner, the doorbell rings and the neighbors, beaming with joy to have you there, deliver a steaming hot homemade meal for you in containers you don't have to return.

I didn't expect San Francisco to roll out the red carpet when we arrived, but I did expect a friendlier welcome. A few instances of "Hello" or "Are you new? Welcome, then." That would do. Instead I had to tell people I'd just moved.

Introductions are like checking in at the counter for a doctor's appointment, greeting a colleague at a meeting, telling the waiter what you want from the menu. We start somewhere. Let's start with, "Hi, my name is ____. What's yours?" Introductions bring us back to the basics of starting over, starting anew. We are made for one another. Jane Jacobs said this about neighbors:

> The first fundamental of successful city life: People must take a modicum of responsibility for each other even if they have no ties to each other. This is a lesson no one learns by being told. It is learned from the experience of having other people without ties of kinship or close friendship or formal responsibility to you take a modicum of responsibility for you.[1]

Neighbors might not be your BFFs, but they're your wall-sharers, your fence-sharers. God might have more for these relationships, but you've got to start the introductions. "Better is a neighbor who is near than a brother who is far away" (Prov. 27:10). In living sent, we go to our neighbors to make the introductions. Differences might be quite obvious. The decor, the social status, the scents. But we are suburb and city dwellers of faith. We start the trust test. Let them see they can depend on us. Imagine: What if we all did just that? Our communities would have strong ties of woven trust.

Each move grants us the opportunity to start over and start introductions. If this didn't happen upon arrival, remember living sent is a lifestyle. We can put into practice today cultivating an awareness of neighbors, making introductions, and mapping out where they live. I discovered that introducing myself and our family locked us into a habit of meeting people and sharing stories.

We've lived in three homes during our time in San Francisco. I don't wear these as badges of honor. If you've moved even once in your life and lived to tell about it, you know you've told yourself what I did with each move: "I'm never doing that again!"

351 King Street (Downtown Apartment)

Our first home was in a very transient neighborhood. It made sense to live there first. We initially signed a one-year lease but stayed eighteen months. It was in this apartment that we lived out our first thirty-one days. We hosted a BBQ in the outdoor commons area. We reached out to our next-door neighbors, and it was while eating dinner out with them one night that they told us they were expecting their first child. We got to know the concierge and maintenance guys. One would think with a mailroom that serves over five hundred residents we'd see the same faces there daily, but that was rare. We did see what everyone tossed as junk mail. It pained us when this included our church invite cards.

Apartment living affords introverts heavy, spring-loaded doors that shut immediately. Apartment living also affords extroverts amenities like a gym, grill, and pool area. It was on those nights when the fire alarm rattled the building that we got to interact with the introverts. It was on our walks that we got to know the rest of our community.

Living thousands of miles from where we grew up, it was an out-of-body experience to hear a stranger shout, "Roll Tide!" to us one Saturday morning as we returned from the grocery store. We looked down and all around to discover that our youngest was wearing his older brother's hand-me-down University of Alabama shirt. The stranger who'd shouted was beaming. He'd found something in common with us. I didn't think I'd ever say "Roll Tide" on the West Coast, but it stumbled out of our mouths back to him. This was followed by a handshake and name exchange. We each pointed out where we lived and got to share our stories of how we'd ended up in San Francisco. Does anyone else say "Roll Tide" in this city? Maybe. Regardless, when you start with who you are, then you'll start to like where you live. You'll find pieces of life around you that God will use to make you smile as profound reminders that He sees you and cares for you.

524 Day Street (Cozy Block)

For over a year, on our drive across the city to the kids' school, we'd ask God for favor in the neighborhood and to help us find a place to live near their school. It was through another crazy encounter with Craigslist that Ben became the first to respond to a newly listed rental house. I'll leave out the bumps and bruises of getting out of our lease and moving across town, for the point of this chapter is the neighbors we would meet, not the gray hairs I would accumulate. One of the neighborly encounters that we brought with us across town was delivering gift bags to the nine houses on our dead-end road where less than twenty-five other people lived. We now had a backyard with an apple tree and a lemon tree. When God gives you lemons, give them away—and add your contact information so you can be that family neighbors can call upon in times of trouble or for cups of sugar. The welcome committee didn't parade around us at this home either, but the bags of lemons plus cookies and contact information were well received. Except by one man. He cracked his door open after little hands banged on it. Cracked it open a little wider just to slide his hand out and receive the bag. Nothing said. Door shut. Okay, then.

The home was on one of San Francisco's many hills, which gave us all viewing rights into each other's yards. Our neighbors heard our kids argue, bought cups of lemonade our kids would sell, and shared veggies from their gardens. It was on this street and with these neighbors that we hosted a homemade arcade and homemade ice cream social, invited a new family over for brunch, and made meals for an elderly neighbor after he returned from the hospital. We started a gathering we called "Cookies and Cocoa" at Christmastime as my way of baking all the important sweets without having to eat all of them. Sharing was far more fun. The kids made invite cards and delivered them to the nine homes. Some neighbors were forced to talk to one another even though they didn't like each other.

We loved the people on this street very much. But staying was taken away from us when the landlord decided to put the house up for sale, its price way beyond our means. Where would we go now? Our kids went to school in this neighborhood and played sports here. We were just starting to feel settled after two years in this home. Well, we must have had new neighbors to meet. That's the looking-for-Jesus approach. The self-absorbed one was quite lengthy, and was wadded up in a tissue of tears at His feet.

126 Cayuga Ave. (Bustling Street)

I will forever say we got our new home by circling it in prayer. I put Mark Batterson's approach into action but chose to drive rather than walk around this potential home. I wanted this home and needed to pray aloud. I didn't want to ward off the potential neighbors by doing so on foot. It felt safer and less ostracizing in the van. I couldn't see all that God could see in this place, but it met the need for our growing family, as we would soon bring home Kavita, our adopted daughter from India. It was near public transit for Ben and the freeway was quickly accessible to take the kids all over the city.

Within the first week, we made introductions with our bags of cookies and contact information. God didn't give us lemons with this house. Our annual Cookies and Cocoa continued, and now we had many more neighbors to invite. Hundreds walk by our home on foot commute, and dozens of company buses pass by. After we moved in, we learned we now lived above a creek that would occasionally flood parts of our neighborhood. While we weren't directly affected, we took meals of focaccia and soup. Our kids didn't leave their backyard arguments behind at the other house on the hill. As I spent more time with our blue-house neighbors, they told me how much they enjoyed hearing the kids outside. "It reminds us of our boys when we first moved here in the early eighties." These would also be the neighbors who would share their summer plums and hem our clothes.

Our family hosted a neighborhood pizza night that was a huge success. I'll tell you more about the pizza night later on, but I still have one regret about living in this current neighborhood: I didn't throw Mr. Sanchez a party.

If I had known Mr. Sanchez when I was circling our home in prayer, I would have felt far more comfortable talking out loud on the street. It's what he did every day. I confess that we called him "crazy man" for several weeks, until we realized he had a name and it wasn't the one we had given him. I approached another neighbor to get the scoop on "crazy man," only to learn his name was Mr. Sanchez and he was an older man who lived with his even older parents. The state didn't know what to do with him. Neither did his parents. So, most days he walked up and down the street hollering at the buses and foot commuters, unless he was stoned. Then he'd take a nap in the afternoon sun, propped up against our fence. It would be Ben who picked up the Spanish Mr. Sanchez spoke, and they often conversed at the end of the day.

I wanted him to feel loved and thought about throwing him a party, but after returning from a summer trip I noticed our neighborhood was missing his voice. I asked a few neighbors. One learned from a clerk at the grocery store that he had died. My mind immediately went to the party I had been planning. I envisioned a very long table with many balloons and Mr. Sanchez at the head. Nothing extravagant. Set up in our driveway. Laughter and conversation in abundance.

I've tried not to hang my head in guilt for not fulfilling this dream I had for him, but by learning his name and speaking to him when others avoided him, we did celebrate him. Because of Mr. Sanchez's life, I'm more committed than ever to be party throwers in our neighborhood. The night we first served pizza we were right where Mr. Sanchez would catch his afternoon naps.

This Is Real

Our neighbors and coworkers have names, and we need to know them. They have stories, and we need to listen. We have a God who loves us, and they have the same God who loves them. This is no longer hypothetical. You're still close to home—haven't ventured out too far yet. Whether you are new to town or new to this lifestyle, you've started to stay and now you're seeing what's right around you - your neighbors, God's plan, the enemy's tactics, and God's presence. As we're learning to love where we live, fear has less and less control. Make those introductions. We can talk to people, because they are who we are here to love.

Kevin McAllister, in *Home Alone*, conquers his fear of an unknown knock at the door by proclaiming outside his house, "Hey, I'm not afraid anymore. I said I'm not afraid anymore." (Until the snow-shoveling neighbor approaches. Then he runs to hide under his parents' bedcovers.)

We have a family motto: "Be you. Don't hide you. Be you." We want our neighbors to be themselves, and we're going to give them the same. Here are a few ways we live this out with our neighbors on our block:

- Purchase 100 percent of the food from Costco and spread it out and call it gourmet.
- With some couples, we always dine at a restaurant. Always. And we're fine with that.
- Invite their kids over. We give permission for our kids to hide their LEGO creations that took hours to build, but get every other toy out. Put on a movie and pop some popcorn for the kids so the adults can talk for longer than five minutes.
- Talk about schools. It's what they know well, and we've got a thing or two to learn.
- They built their home out of an earthquake shelter that was constructed after 1906. They've added on over the years. We've taken tours many times, and he beams brighter each time he gets to show it off. Plus, we would trade apples for

Name your neighbors.

potatoes, artichokes, and cauliflower from our gardens. It's never been a fair trade.

- This fellow is Jewish and reminds us of the older gentleman from the movie *Up*. He does Sabbath well and dances religiously every Friday night.

Like most appointments, you return for further check-ups. When you return to a restaurant, you look over the menu for new and different entrees. The same principle applies to engagement with our neighbors. The introductions are a start, but we keep checking in. We keep inquiring about what's new and different in their lives and on the street. Our family is no longer the new kids on the block. We're the welcoming committee. In living sent, we're the ones who connect neighbors to one another. The longer dwellers of faith call a street or neighborhood *home*, the stronger the potential for community to form.

Make a list of the neighbors you know that live near you. Maybe you only can describe them for now until you learn their names. Start the introductions, no matter how long you've lived there. I highly recommend lemons and cookies and contact cards.

DWELLER TIP

Every city block or neighborhood will have an unofficial mayor. Someone who's been there a long time, likely seen a lot of change, and constantly has eyes on the street. Get to know them. Their wealth of stories will give you incredible context for the city you love.

—Carmen, realtor in Atlanta

9

Meet the Faith Family

I've never had to find a church. I've never had the opportunity to shop around. I haven't gotten to bail when it got hard. I've had to endure church business meetings in my younger days and keep my ugly words inside when anyone was unkind to my pastor dad or pastor husband. That just comes standard with the job. What also comes standard is that Jesus continues to build His church, and nothing will stop it!

The Most Welcoming Place on the Planet

Despite not having to find one, I'd choose my church over any other gathering or organization any day. I believe in the local church. I advertise for it. I do my share of inviting. For I am convinced that our faith communities are the central hub for empowering us to love where we live and live out His love.

In living sent, we set out the largest welcome mat at the doors of our churches. A place where everyone feels at home and is open to inviting others in. The church is commissioned by Christ to carry out His mission until He returns. What we lack individually, God gives us through the church, and when the church is functioning under God Almighty, then His kingdom will come and His will be done on earth as it is in heaven. Step into it to see it.

The church is not made up of a perfect family but a useful one. A living, breathing, thriving organism that is responsive to God's activity around us and beyond. The church fulfills the Scriptures of loving the least of these, training and equipping the people, meeting needs, and teaching sound doctrine. People are progressing in their relationship with Jesus because of the church. This is foundational.

Now, while we don't look like one another, we love one another. We have different backgrounds and upbringings but face the future with the same hope. It's the people of the church who have celebrated with me, dropped by to cheer me up, and prayed over me. "By this all people will know that you are my disciples, if you have love for one another" (John 13:35). Jesus intends for His followers to care for each other, and by doing so, the world will see and want to be a part of it.

Introductions happen here as in the neighborhood—welcoming in new people and showing happiness that others are back again. The faith family is growing close to one another but is not closed off to others.

I remember Ben meeting my family for the first time, and I remember meeting his. It was extremely vulnerable and awkward, but we did so because there's nothing like getting attached. On the other side of awkward and vulnerable deep breaths are waiting. Muster up the courage, take a deep breath, and exhale. For what we have in common is far greater than our differences.

Brian Zahnd, dweller and pastor in Missouri, paints this picture for us: "Imagine. A watcher from another world. Sees all of human history. His conclusion? 'Poor things, they don't know they're all in this together.'"[1]

Be a part of a faith family you can invite others to come to with you. Having a church to invite others to is a massive tool in living sent. If you don't feel comfortable inviting a friend, a neighbor, or anyone to your church, I would urge you to reevaluate why you're there. God desires to grow His kingdom, and He's set up the church to do so—a local body that is welcoming and growing.

My dad would pray on Sundays, as the benediction was given, "And may we be Your people scattered as we leave this *place*." This place being the church, and the people those who are intended to carry His story of grace throughout our days, until we met again. I could picture us scattering while standing there with my teenaged eyes closed, holding on to the pew. I just couldn't have pictured what its results would be.

Faith Family Cures Isolation

We had lived in San Francisco for only a few months. Our family was at Old Navy for their $10 jean sale on a Friday night. As I came out of the dressing area with the boys, there standing by Ben was our church staff. Here's what I knew:

> They were not there to get $10 jeans or fashion tips from me.
> This city was big, and them being there wasn't a coincidence.
> There was no, "Hey, what are you doing here?"
> Or, "Well, what a small world!"

They needed us. They needed to be standing beside us, be it at an Old Navy or a Waffle House. (We don't have those in San Francisco, but I could sure go for one about 11:00 p.m. some nights.) They needed to not feel alone in a crowded, new place.

Ben and I said nothing to each other. We didn't have to. I made my way to the cashier and bought our pile of jeans. As I finished the transaction, Ben said, "We can't leave them."

He was right. Ben and I certainly weren't the wisest and strongest in the bunch, but in the moment, we knew they were looking at us to tell them what was next.

"Let's get ice cream. Our treat," Ben told the group with confidence. It was as if he had solved the world's problems. And to be honest, to the six of us adults, he had.

We were learning the streets and knew that going out the door to the right would take us back to our apartments, so we went left. We walked to where every tourist in the city flocks—Union Square. Remember, we had yet to discover the amazing bakeries, restaurants, and coffee shops. In a sense, we were still tourists but trying not to look like it.

Ben took us to the basement of the massive Macy's. We passed by the Kitchen-Aids on sale and Boudin's bread bowls and went straight to Ben and Jerry's. Everyone put in their order. I watched as my thirty-three-year-old husband stepped up to the role of leader and forerunner. It's as if we were college students and Dad was in town for a visit. He paid for nine ice creams and got that many thank-yous.

We went back outside with our treats and corralled some chairs at Union Square. The skyscrapers loomed large around us. Thousands of different noises caught our attention from time to time. We were speaking English, but no one else that walked by us was. We thoroughly enjoyed our ice cream and each other's presence. All seemed well now. It was good to be together. To be reminded that we had to start somewhere, and that starting is often the hardest part.

I looked at everyone. No one was saying it, but we were all thinking the same thing. *I want my mom and I want this to be easier, but Ben and Jerry's will do!*

Years from that moment, I can chuckle every time I see Ben and Jerry's ice cream in the freezer section or find myself at the flagship Old Navy store on 4th and Market. A faith community is the cure for isolation, paralysis, and seclusion. It was that evening for the nine of us.

Family forms in the church, and when it does, isolation shrivels up and dies. We want to be together because we've lived the other days out in the city. It's best to live our days out in the community so that we can bring others into the church to experience what we have together. It's a coming home each time we're together.

Faith Family Connects to Community

What began with the start of our church is still present today. A family has been formed in the local church. Perhaps more so because we have all moved far from biological family. When friends become family, we begin to see ourselves where we live long term. When we experience life together, we create memories. Memories are links—links to our town and to the people of our community. I can call friends and family who live elsewhere, but they can't fully grasp life here because they aren't in the everyday with me. In my corner of the world, my fellow citizens and I understand each other because we're smelling the same stuff on the streets, interacting with the same culture, and cheering for the same teams. Well, most of us are.

Bob and Cecile relocated to live close to their sons. They were a part of a megachurch in southern California and wouldn't feel settled until they found a new church home. Bob came to our church one Sunday and returned home to tell Cecile that they had a new church family and he couldn't wait to take her next week.

Victor moved from Spain to the city months before his wife, Lidia, and their two daughters joined him. Lidia's only request was a faith family. She had no thoughts on their home or furniture or school—at least not yet. He was delighted to call her and report he had done as she requested.

Dalen and Stephanie were church folk who traded coasts and lifestyles. Full-time work to full-time work plus a child. As they found their faith community, they let the church leadership know they were ready to serve and started hosting a small group. The same was true with Tim and Laura Ann. They knew their stay would be short but would also be meaningless without the local church. She took her musical talent straight to the worship team, and they hosted a small group and led faithfully until God called them back east.

Faith Families Live Commissioned as One

"There is one body and one Spirit—just as you were called to the one hope that belongs to your call—one Lord, one faith, one baptism, one God and Father of all, who is over all and through all and in all" (Eph. 4:4–6). A beautiful reminder that it's not you and me and them, but we're all one.

Rees Howells, founder of the Bible College of Wales, said, "Duties varied, but their commission as one."[2] In our faith community, there are as many walks of life as occupations as countries represented. Yet our vision in the local church is clear: to see an increasing number of San Franciscans orient their entire lives around Jesus. We are diverse and at different places on our faith journey, but our goal is the same. "There are times in God's dealings with His servants when He sets apart for Himself not just individuals but companies—baptized, as it were, by one spirit into one body for one God-appointed purpose."[3]

God sets us apart as individuals but calls us into community in one Spirit and in one body and with one Lord, so that we might be about His kingdom here on earth. Londoner Tricia Neill, president of Alpha International and a part of Holy Trinity Church Brompton, says this about the faith family: "With the participation of the whole congregation, a church can afford a bigger vision."[4]

Once you've found this welcome mat in your town, introduce yourself to the leadership. They'll be delighted to have you, and you'll be a part of making the vision of His church a reality in your community.

Faith Families Embrace Crazy

I've yet to meet a fun family that doesn't also have an element of crazy. We're learning in our faith community that God wants to do a fresh work in His church in this generation. He wants to do immeasurably more through the conduit of His church. When we're open to Him, His Word, and His world, the crazy happens!

A tweet one Sunday afternoon particularly caught Ben's attention. He reached out to the writer, Alan Clayton, and they met for coffee. Ben got to know Alan's story. His work brought him across the pond from his homeland of Ireland to the United States and Asia. Now, when he's in San Francisco, he comes to our church. He comes over to our home for dinner. He's a part of a small group, a part of our faith family.

God drew Alan into our church through Ben's teachings, authentic hospitality, accessible worship, and the fellowship of others. He said so. He left on Sundays ready to merge his faith with his work. He was experiencing the incredible way God infuses us with His Spirit—to speak and live in a way that bridges our belief in God to our gifts and passions. For Alan, it was God using his passion of resourcing start-ups. But this was what Alan was seeing God do on his work trips. What was happening back in his hometown in Ireland? God was doing something significant in Alan's heart toward his community. His coastal town was no longer a place where he lived only to consume its beauty and serenity and opportunities. It was becoming a place where he began to ask, "What can I give," rather than "What can I take?"

Alan grew up Protestant. Gwenn, his wife, grew up Catholic. In their married life, they had been a part of diverse churches in the city, remote farming villages, and suburban towns. Church leaders had poured into their marriage and spiritual journeys along the way. As they looked back on their career paths and their leadership opportunities, they could see how God had provided at just the right time. Now they stood together, looking forward and trusting in the same God who had seen them through so much.

With that abundance, Alan and Gwenn graciously invited Ben and me to visit them in Ireland. They introduced us to their life and family and countryside. They invited their friends over to listen to our God story.

Alan and Gwenn, with a fresh awakening in their souls, handed over the lead role to God for their family, home, community, and country. They did their part and watched God do His. In that setting, a small group was born. Together with their friends and family, they were inspired to be the church rather than consider the church to be a place to visit on Sundays only. Add ten friends to the story. Ten friends whom Alan and Gwenn had never shared their faith with before!

Their hearts beat to have "one church, one faith, one Lord" in their town seven days a week. To be singing to the Lord a new song, and not the same song Alan sang as a choirboy! To shine on the lives of young people in their town and to do mission in a place where promoting Christ was mostly thought unnecessary or even unbiblical.

So Alan and Gwenn took this one life they had been given, this one faith they had in God, this one vibrant heart for their community, and their individual and unique giftedness to be on mission with Him.

There's a church community in San Francisco that is praying for their faith family as they grow deep and wide. A church community that Alan Clayton stepped into on a work trip, where he discovered afresh and anew that God is alive and on the move in the local church.

Together Is Better

I love what God gives Jeremiah to tell the people:

> Amend your ways and your deeds, and I will let you dwell in this place . . . if you truly amend your ways and your deeds, if you truly execute justice one with another, if you do not oppress the sojourner, the fatherless, or the widow, or shed innocent blood in

this place, and if you do not go after other gods to your own harm, then I will let you dwell in this place, in the land that I gave of old to your fathers forever. (Jer. 7:3, 5–7)

That's what I want to be a part of! I want our land to be a place where God dwells and gives us to live in and sees thrive. To do this, we must welcome all into the faith family. When we live commissioned as one, the one grows yet stays as one. So point your neighbors, colleagues, and friends to your church. "Christians are Christ's body, the organism through which God works. Every addition to that body enables Him to do more," wrote C. S. Lewis.[5]

We come together to be scattered to come back together. Faith dwellers come to regroup, refuel, and recharge but then return to the people God has called us to reach. Yes, we look to our community leaders and government officials to execute justice and care for the marginalized. But we can also look to the local church embodied by faith dwellers to carry out the Christian mandate to love and serve. If everyone were in the church, then we'd be there all the time. But they're not, so we're not.

Some Sundays, back in my childhood church, we were instructed to hold hands with the people next to us, stretching across the aisles. We'd sing, "I'm so glad I'm a part of the family of God" or "Bind us together, Lord, bind us together with love." In those days, it felt forced upon me, like having to hug dear ole Aunt Sally. Oddly enough, it was these quirky, peculiar, precious people who still come to mind as I think of the family that raised me and poured into me and spoke truth to me. Living scattered has brought me into a faith family on the other side of the country. And though we don't hold hands across the aisle and sing, we greet one another. Those handshakes and hugs infuse a power that carries me to live sent and scattered until we see each other again, knowing we are all trying to love where we live. The faith family is the scattered. The awakened. They hold the record for the largest welcome mat in town. Find one, if you haven't already. One you can bring your neighbor to. Thank God for the church, His faith family here on Planet Earth.

DWELLER TIP

When asked about your weekend in the workplace, don't leave out church! Share why it's special to you. This is even a great way to find out if you work with other Christians.

—Justin, e-commerce product manager

essentials on hand

• • • • • •

*He has shown you, O mortal, what is good. And what does the L*ORD *require of you? To act justly and to love mercy and to walk humbly with your God.*

Micah 6:8 NIV

10

Walking Shoes

An "aha" moment for me in regard to shoes happened in the first few days of living in the city. I realized the necessity for taking shoes off just inside the house. It had never made sense beforehand. Why would you take off your shoes? What if your feet smelled? If you're a dinner guest, isn't it a little too comfortable to walk around someone's home in just socks, or even worse, bare feet? I had lived most of my life in towns where you got places by car—where my shoes didn't step in what they were stepping in now, around the city. I get it now. Kindly leave your shoes at the door. I welcome mismatched socks, holey socks, and your lovely bare feet.

Shoes Can Have Two Purposes

To some, shoes are accessories. They add height, color, and pizzazz to the outfit. To others, they are necessities. They provide the basics of comfort and wearability. You might be one who exchanges your "getting there" shoes for your "working there" shoes. Occasionally, the shoe business makes a shoe that fits both purposes well, where they add to the outfit and are comfortable to walk in. I have a few pair in that category.

Now, my shoes probably aren't your shoes. My Southern California friends can walk 365 days in their Birkenstocks. My Seattle friends tend to live in their rain boots. My go-to shoes are my brown boots. Even on the Fourth of July. Especially on the Fourth of July, in the foggy city by the bay.

Regardless of our shoe tastes, we can all testify that a good pair of walking shoes is a must for living sent. Dwellers, it doesn't take long to learn this lesson the hard way. Blisters will be your initiation fee. Of all the essentials, this is the most expensive and worth every penny. Our feet take us through neighborhoods, down streets, and into buildings.

Whatever your shoe choice, I need you to slide them on. Lace them up. We're going on a walk. The first person we'll meet up with is Ruth.

Ruth and I met at a prayer experience at our church, and I asked about her story. I knew I could understand it better if I let her show me around her neighborhood, the Tenderloin, known for its theaters, music halls, and sketchy sidewalk interactions. Ruth is street smart. She has walked enough at all hours of the day to know who's got her back and what streets to avoid at what times. She used to live as close to police stations as possible to keep herself and her children safe. I observed Ruth as much as I did my surroundings. She had a pep in her step as she proudly led me up and down Turk, Ellis, and Eddy Street. She had met Jesus in her neighborhood, gotten clean, and gotten off the streets. It was obvious, and not just to me. She knew every shop owner and passerby by name.

"Hi, Dana." She'd then whisper to me, "That girl is legit."

"What's up, Bobby?" She'd point out that he had been clean for some time now.

"This is Carolyn. She is a nurse at our ministry center."

I'm the one who walked timidly and on guard. But I was walking with Ruth, and that made all the difference. She was teaching me how to walk.

Ruth took me to the ministry center in the neighborhood, which I was familiar with because our church partners with them. She then walked me to my minivan parked in her neighborhood. She held out her arm to slow me down as we crossed the street. I was worried she saw the parking meter man. (You know me and tickets.) She was concerned about a man who was peering into my van window. We watched him for a minute. He wore a suit with a bright blue shirt and a winter hat. It appeared he was using the window as a mirror as he tidied himself up, put on his winter hat, and smoothed lotion on his hands. We got a little closer, but Ruth still kept some distance. Now he was trying to remove a pendant from a chain using a very large kitchen knife. Ruth told me he could barter on the streets with two items better than one.

"Okay." This was a whole new world for me. I was paying close attention and found myself holding Ruth's hand.

I let her do all the talking at first. We learned his name was Salem. His speech was hard to understand. We gathered that he needed a friend and Ruth told him about City Impact, a ministry in the neighborhood. She then prayed for him. Her heart was breaking for her neighbor. My heart was troubled for my neighbor as well.

Salem told us he had built trust and then his "friends" took advantage of him. That's why he hates that he even trusts at all. Salem had six cell phones taken from him. He struggled to speak. His mouth watered as he talked to us. He dabbed it with a red cloth. He shared with us that he had been a preacher once and got into some debt, and that led to foolish decisions. He went to prison for bank robbery and lost everything.

He went back to working on his project with the large kitchen knife. We gave each other a despairing look. Before I left, I wanted to pray with Ruth as she had prayed with Salem.

He overheard me pray about Ruth's marriage and a retreat coming up, and then he told us both that you're not really married until you learn to take on your spouse's struggles and heartache. Whoa! He said that so clearly too. Salem wasn't done telling us his story. He was married for thirty-five years. He spoke of Jesus and Moses, and that God gives us struggles so that we can walk through them and know Him more. I told him that though he has a hard time with his speech, he can preach! I told him that he had stories to share, and that I wanted to find him again and give him a journal and pen for him to write down his stories. He said he loved to write. I told him I did too!

· · · · · · ·

Meet Patricia. She lives in Switzerland. The first time I met her, she and her husband had come to our church while in town for a conference. She understands how to live sent and knows to pack the essentials when she visits another place. On another one of her visits, Patricia stopped by our church's weekday small group for community and inspiration. Several people commented on her good pair of walking shoes. She told us that since her last visit, she had heard about the Tenderloin, a neighborhood she had yet to explore. Patricia had plans to go on an intentional walk to pray and learn. She probably walked right by Salem.

· · · · · · ·

This is Candace and Rusty. They've learned how to walk together. So much of their new life has been a drive-by, until they adjusted their daily schedule. They have chosen to wake up thirty minutes earlier, giving them time to walk to work more slowly. They inhale and exhale and practice His presence. This empty-nester couple prays differently because they see as they walk. They are drawn to pray for city officials and the sanitation department. They ask God to infuse integrity and wisdom into our leaders. They are calling on God to raise up believers into positions of influence. They meet people in their complex, at the cafe, and around their neighborhood. They're building relationships and having people over for dinner because of where their walking shoes take them. They haven't called this city home for long, but their love for this place is deeper than most. It started with intercession, and regardless of how long God has them here, this place will be different because He heard and responded to two hearts who walked the city in an ongoing conversation with Him.

· · · · · ·

God kind of makes a big deal out of walking. In the Old Testament, God made mention when His people walked faithfully, obediently, and wisely. Enoch, Noah, Abraham, and Isaac are some of the people who were accredited with such faith walks. They walked through northern Africa and the Middle East. Because Pharaoh's daughter was walking by the river, Moses was discovered in the floating basket (Exod. 2:5). Ironically, later in life, Moses walked through the Red Sea across dry land, leading millions to freedom (15:19).

In the New Testament, Jesus walked on water. He made the lame walk. He taught parables and discipled His twelve close friends as he walked. Jesus walked in the country and through the crowds. From the very beginning, God has walked with us: "I will walk among you and will be your God, and you shall be my people" (Lev. 26:12).

A Tale of Two Walks

We can walk to add to our life or to simply get from point A to point B. Our walks through our towns and communities can be marked as steps of faith, believing that God has called us, sent us, and has purpose on every street and around every corner.

In the parable of the Good Samaritan, the priest and the Levite were also walking, just not the same way as the Samaritan. All three saw the same thing—a man left half-dead on the road. The priest had most likely just come from church, and the Levite knew God's law very well. Yet both avoided God on the street that day by switching to the other side. On their walk, the priest and Levite knew what they saw and knew what to do, but they chose convenience and resisted compassion. They walked away from the hurt. The Samaritan walked over to the man. He walked away from convenience and into compassion. His walking feet would continue to meet a need as he helped him up and into deeper care. In this parable, all three were deliberate in their walking.

Walking brings us to intersections of joining God at work where we live, of seeing what He sees and extending compassion. Not just when it's convenient. Most often when it's not. Let's not overanalyze where we are walking, simply pay attention. We see into our city when we walk our city. We touch the city rather than keep sanitized in our cars. If we don't know our communities, it is because we're not out in them. The people we walk beside are not "them" but "us." Take it from the wisest man who ever lived: "The heart of man plans his way, but the LORD establishes his steps" (Prov. 16:9).

How to Best Use Your Good Pair of Walking Shoes

Walk to Learn

Once you're a citizen of a town, you share the streets. Tourists just borrow them. So do a deeper work with your fellow neighbors. I'm convinced we learn more from walking our streets than driving through them. We see details and make discoveries. If your city is walkable, thank the urban planners.

Go for a walk. Observe the people. The buildings. Imagine what's taking place inside. Our walks have taught us to pray over any storefront with wrought-iron bars on its windows, for it could be a sex trafficking location. What shoes do you have that can get you through your town? Wear the soles out of them. Make them your Ebenezer stones, a physical reminder of a spiritual truth.

Take inventory of your streets. Go back to your map. Draw and name the streets that you walk down or need to walk down. If you don't know the names, etch the landmarks.

Walk to Celebrate

Breathe in what gives life and exhale what gives thanks. Celebrate what we have in common; yes, even our differences. Especially our differences. I've grown an appreciation in my adulthood for Shakespeare, opera, oysters, and Vietnamese coffee as I celebrated life with others.

Find your favorite places to walk. Discover a new part of town. The Presidio hiking trails are like a cool misty shower. My feet pounce on the spongy brown land. I've forgotten all about my shoes. Eucalyptus has taken over my senses. Walking, especially among natural beauty, helps us anyway. It can lower stress, give us fresh air to breathe in, and make us more attuned to our surroundings.[1] What is walkable for you?

Walk to Pray

Step foot on the places He's giving you. Among the eucalyptus trees until the trail opens up to the ocean. Through the rough part of town, into a cafe for a brioche donut and cup of tea. What part of the city doesn't have your footprints? The dark and broken areas, the up-and-coming neighborhoods, the natural paths? Consider them your prayer ground and start walking.

As you walk, let this word picture of praise come alive: "The earth is the LORD's and the fullness thereof, the world and those who dwell therein, for he has founded it upon the seas and established it upon the rivers" (Ps. 24:1–2).

Prayer walking is a powerful tactic for every dweller. What part of your city needs God's intervention? Where do you sense darkness? Where do you sense opportunity? I prayer walked around our home before it was ours. In a city where multiple cash offers are made on each property for sale, I knew it would take a miracle of God for us to get it. We prayer walk around our schools the Saturday before the start of school every year. It's a moving and active declaration that the building, the staff, the students, the conversations, the academia are entrusted into His care. We claim God's protection and truth over the entire block and school year.

Before we moved to the city, we invited fifteen church leaders to meet us in San Francisco to walk and pray with us in the neighborhoods along the bay. We walked by condemned warehouses, lots overgrown with weeds, and chain-link fences. We believed God for what we couldn't even see. Today a women's and children's hospital and the Golden State Warriors arena sit in these lots that were covered in prayer.

Prayer walking merges "me" and "them." It allows us to walk toward compassion. What will be *your* next Good Samaritan story? No one knows the names of these men in the biblical account. Just that one was good and the other was in need. That's enough. Nothing more is needed. We lace up our shoes daily to make His name known, not our own. But when we lift Him up, we will draw others to Him. What part of town needs to hear the name of Jesus? Walk there and speak His name.

DWELLER TIP

Invite someone on a walk around the neighborhood followed by brunch or lunch! Share your love for where you live.

—Minnie L.

11

Seeing Eyes

We were that family who had just arrived, with a few days to get "settled in." I saw people in a hurry, and that made me feel late. I didn't even have somewhere to be! I watched couples and families in their routine, handing off lunches and kisses, and realized we didn't have the luxury of leaving one another. When you're new, you can't help but see. I stared at the majestic coastline covered in a chill that beckoned fire pits rather than fashionable summer gear. Wealth and poverty coexisted on the sidewalks. I noticed the city was constructing new, better, taller, more sustainable, eco-friendly buildings, bridges, and roadways. If my eyes hadn't taken in enough on our walks around the neighborhood, they went cross-eyed watching my kids, who were dominating the sidewalk in zig-zag formations. I apologized to the business folk with their fancy bags and earbuds as they dodged my littles. I saw people like me and not like me. Everything was gray. Concrete gray. Oh, and the crosswalk signals. My eyes glazed over, waiting for the image of the person to appear and the countdown to begin. Would we make it? was always the question with three kids in tow. My physical eyes were taking in so much of this new place that I'd collapse in bed exhausted just from seeing.

What Being New Lets Us See

Being new is just as hip as wearing the "hello" nametag or con-ference lanyard on day two. Newbies are handed the excuse of just moving to a place on a silver platter with an expiration date determined by the local community. Everything has its new car smell and is still in the packaging.

Being new affords us countless privileges and an equal number of headaches. It's both these privileges and the headaches that make for great stories. The headaches maybe more so! Being new gives us fresh eyes. Being new is like having a clean pair of shoes that are leaving the carpet for the first time and stepping outside. And God can do wonders with fresh eyes and clean shoes on the ground.

Friends of ours, who relocated to Manhattan a year before we traded the Midwest for the West Coast, told us that taking in a new culture would initially wear us out. It would strip us of self, revealing our need for Jesus. They were right. San Francisco wore me out in two ways. First was pure exhaustion from taking in so many sights and sounds and signs. Noises, people, and directions. Second was a prophetic word from these Manhattan dwellers. Moving with the purpose of living sent makes us vulnerable.

I'll put it this way. For me to go camping—as in sleeping bags, community bathrooms, cooking over a fire and such—is beyond my comfort zone. I'm all five senses, paying attention to everything below my feet and every sound around me, all I touch and see. I'm fully awake, not on autopilot, because I'm in unfamiliar territory. This affords me a strong memory bank and sharp eyesight that routine campers and park returnees might not have. It's become normal and familiar for them.

This same privilege is for those who have uprooted and re-planted in a different environment. Be it across town, closer to work, to the other side of the state, or to a different coast, country, or outlook, a change of place shuffles our senses. The air feels different. The routes, foliage, and landmarks have changed, and we're taking in new sights. So before we try to get life back to normal as quickly as possible, let's see what God wants us to see and depend upon Him, not ourselves.

Look Up before You Look Out

With this lifestyle, I've learned it is extremely helpful to take care of yourself at home before you leave for the day. Fill your mind with God's truth, lay down your burdens, and open yourself up to Him. You will have less baggage to carry with you and will be able to see more clearly. All the more, look up before you look out. See God for who He is—the Author of your life, the Perfecter of your faith, the One who fashioned you and loves you. Look in before you begin. Agree with Him before you leave home that He has given you purpose and a day to rejoice in. Then ask our sending God to show you what He wants you to see. The odds of being intentional in your day are higher when you look up. Leave anxiety and preoccupation at the door. Put on those seeing eyes, for we've got a place and a people to notice. This lifestyle requires that you be out and about and notice your surroundings.

Seeing God

Elisha saw one army and his servant saw another. The servant saw a vast amount of horses and chariots surrounding the city. Elisha, though he knew what was physically present, saw what God saw: "Do not be afraid, for those who are with us are more than those who are with them" (2 Kings 6:16). I believe what God did for Elisha in prayer can be done in our vision for where we live. He prayed, "O LORD, please open his eyes that he may see." The servant then saw what Elisha and God saw: "and behold, the mountain was full of horses and chariots of fire all around Elisha" (v. 17). This might be your prayer, or the prayer you are praying for those in your faith community. The difference between fear and faith has everything to do with what we see. Faith is the assurance of what we do *not* see. Take it from Moses, who was accredited for persevering because he saw Him who is invisible. And He *is* greater than anything else in this world. We'll see that when we see with eyes of faith.

Wide-Eyed Wonder

The kind of eyesight Christ gives is wide-eyed wonder. The alternative is tunnel vision, which is a singular focus. I pass by many tunnel visionaries a day. Oh, they're accomplishing much for the world in their field with their expertise in their time. This type of vision is stellar in many aspects of life, but not in living sent. Tunnel vision causes us to miss out on what's around us. With wide-eyed wonder, I see the guy smoking marijuana to my left, the cyclist coming up on my right, the parade in front of me, and the flashing emergency vehicle lights behind me. But this is just the start. God desires to show us the stories behind the sights—the depths in all dimensions.

A wide-eyed wonder moment happened for Peter, James, and John when Jesus was transfigured, and Moses and Elijah were on the mountain too. So much goodness. After all they had seen and heard, Jesus came and touched them, and He beckoned them to rise and have no fear. When they lifted their eyes, they saw no one but Jesus only (Matt. 17:1–8).

Nathanael and Philip saw Him with wide-eyed wonder too. "Come and see," said Philip to Nathanael.

"How do you know me?" Nathanael asked Jesus.

"Before Philip called you, when you were under the fig tree, I saw you," Jesus replied. "You will see greater things than these" (John 1:46–50).

It's like Jesus to wow us with His presence and open our eyes. Our eyes were created for dimensional sight, beyond the ordinary, into the realm where God is colliding heaven and earth. This practice takes time. I can attest that the more you use your eye muscles, the sharper they become.

Seeing Eyes

"Seeing eyes" might sound redundant, but we are given physical eyes that don't always see. Have you ever said, "I didn't see that?" Treat your eyes as a superpower. Not everyone will see your town like you; you will not see it like others.

Jordyn uses her superpower well. She moved to our city right after college to work in tech. Her bucket list makes mine look dull. If I don't see her on Sundays, I know she's having a grand adventure and is probably somewhere skiing, hiking, or whitewater rafting. Jordyn had a few things on her list to figure out as she made the city home. She had to learn her weekday walk to the bus stop, how to navigate the grocery store, and scout out the best restaurants in town. Jordyn did this with her white cane in hand and her superpowers in full use.

On the elevator in her apartment building one Sunday morning, she asked the gentleman present what he was doing. His name was Cory, and he told her he was headed to church. She asked more about it, and for the address. And so Jordyn showed up for our noon service. She wasted no time in setting fear aside and using her superpowers to find a place to belong and a people to do life with.

Alertness Is the New Eyesight

Alertness is a keen awareness of our surroundings and the people that fill it. In God's kingdom and with His eyesight, we can envision what has yet to take place here on earth. That's how we live by faith. Jehoshaphat heard from others that great armies were coming against him. He became afraid, and mark what he did next. He "set his face to seek the LORD, and proclaimed a fast throughout all Judah" (2 Chron. 20:3). This is why we fix our eyes on Jesus, because we will face obstacles and opportunities every day of living sent. Jehoshaphat did what most of us would do and talked among his friends, figuring out what to do and recalling what God had done in the past. Then he led this prayer: "We do not know what to do, but our eyes are on you" (v. 12). Oh yes! Job was known by the obstacles he faced, yet he could say, "I had heard of you by the hearing of the ear, but now my eye sees you" (Job 42:5).

The word *alertness* implies a wide-awake attitude, as of someone keenly aware of his or her surroundings, says dictionary.com. Dwellers of faith use this alertness to see what God is doing, to serve where God leads. We strike up a conversation. The weather usually works as a topic. We look for commonalities. Smile. Learn names. If God is planning more for that moment, we walk into it. This is richly satisfying.

Awareness Gives Way to Obedience

Alertness opens awareness. If you've gotten used to life where you live, now is the time to look up before you look out by asking God for a renewal. Also ask those who have just moved to your town what they see. As dwellers of faith, we can break stagnancy with awareness—even if it's borrowed from fresh eyes that help us readjust and gain new vision.

Once your eyes are open, awareness is contagious. You start looking for it. Like a house for sale or flowers you want to grow or a color scheme that delights you, you'll see opportunities all around you. You and I will see differently based on our culture and location. Our unique lens has to do with our current season of life and our God-given personality. Do something with what you see, and don't beat yourself up for what you don't or can't see.

In my corner of the world, I set out to run errands one day before school pick-up and noticed an SUV blocking our entire driveway. This creates a problem when you have no yard to drive through. I had no choice but to call to have the car towed. My imagination told me this was a stolen car that had been dropped off—for this is a common occurrence in our town, and I didn't recognize it as belonging to one of our neighbors. I called. I waited. I went back outside, thinking it had been towed, only to discover the owner of the vehicle had moved it down the street. He was an out-of-towner and apologized. I told him I was glad the tow truck didn't get to his car before he did. Now I was forty minutes late to run errands. I could still fit them in, but I'd need to be fast with no one in my way. You know how that goes! I practically ran into the post office, and a clerk must have seen the talk bubble above my head pleading for another window to open. *Thank you!* We chatted while she prepared my postage label. I asked her if she had anyone affected by the recent hurricanes. She paused. Oh, I didn't need a pause.

"My aunt is on a cruise boat and they are being rerouted in the Caribbean."

She stopped. Oh, gracious. Emotions were present. They'd have to be. A storm was coming. Her aunt was out in it. My eyes were seeing it. My heart was feeling it. It was time to step in, not away. Her tears wet the envelope I had worked so hard to keep Instagram-neat.

"God has the power to make any storm stop and give wisdom to the captain of that ship," I said.

I think she believed me.

"What's your aunt's name?"

I put my hand on top of hers that was on top of the tears that were on top of the envelope.

"While I'm praying for her, will you believe in this God that I speak of?" Our smiles passed through our tightened hand grasp.

If I had been there earlier, she wouldn't have opened the new window. But when God orchestrates an SUV to block your driveway, awareness gives way to obedience. And my soul was thrilled that her tears sealed that envelope for me.

Mark Buchanan, in his book *The Rest of God*, calls this awareness *repentance*. "Repentance is a ruthless dismantling of old ways of seeing and thinking, and then a diligent and vigilant building of new ones. Change begins with fresh eyes, in other words. It begins with an awakened imagination."[1] He goes on to say, "You start to see what God sees, and as God sees it. But that takes more than will. It takes imagination."[2]

Before we close the door of our home behind us, let's look up before we look out. If we look out the door and to our day before we look up to God, we will be overwhelmed by the world's needs and by our own shortcomings. The psalmist guides us out the door: "I lift up my eyes to the hills. From where does my help come? My help comes from the LORD, who made heaven and earth. . . . The LORD will keep your going out and your coming in from this time forth and forevermore" (Ps. 121:1–2, 8).

DWELLER TIP

All moms love a visit to Target! While you're in line grabbing a coffee or in the aisles, strike up a conversation and say hi. At the end of it, tell the mom she's doing a great job! Words of affirmation among mamas go far . . . you might just make her day and give her that extra pep in her step!

—Rachael, mom and avid Target shopper

12

Listening Ears

"This is not who I am."

"I've got everything I need."

"Black lives matter."

"Women's rights are human rights."

"I was here first."

"It's got to be gluten-free, dairy-free."

"Something else has come up. Let's reschedule."

"Put it away. There's kids right here. Hold on."

These statements are what we're saying and what we're hearing. But we use our eyes to see and our ears to hear beyond the obvious and below the surface. In living sent, we are moved by what we encounter and are bothered by what we hear, for we follow God into our communities and He directs us.

· · · · · ·

It was a family affair as we helped hand out groceries to those in need in the Tenderloin neighborhood one August Saturday. This neighborhood of SROs shares a street with Twitter and Uber head-quarters, yet they couldn't be more worlds apart. Through the diligent work of City Impact, we took our SRO assignment and grabbed as many filled grocery bags as our arms could carry. Our boys trusted us and walked with confidence. Ben and I pushed down fear and put on our street-smart faces. I kept reminding myself that the sidewalk is shared space, and I could greet every stranger I passed with a smile. After all, I had groceries in my hands. We let the kids do the first step once we arrived at each resident's door.

"Knock. Knock. City Impact, we have food for you." They said exactly what they were told to say, but in the most precious voices ever. Every door was a surprise. For us and its resident. We had no idea if they would come or could come to the door. If they would trust that we were telling the truth. If they would be adequately dressed and well-behaved. What was true with every opening of the door was the gratefulness on display. After the resident took the bag of groceries, Ben and I would share our first names and ask for theirs. We encountered many Asian residents who didn't understand English and would bow to greet us. We'd graciously bow back to honor them.

Then we'd ask, "How can we pray for you?" Most of the re-sponses were daily needs—money, food, protection, health. Except for Remus.

"Remus, how can we pray for you?"

"That I get more knocks on my door," he said.

I can't even type this story without pausing to pray for Remus again. I give in to the tears that ache for him. Do you hear what he is asking for? He wants to be heard. He wants to be seen. He wants more conversations. Are you listening? Am I listening? Our places cry out. People are hiding, afraid and hungry. Yes, even in quiet, safe neighborhoods. They need to be heard. I want to pray as is written in Lamentations, "Arise, cry out in the night, at the beginning of the night watches! Pour out your heart like water before the presence of the Lord! Lift your hands to him for the lives of your children, who faint for hunger at the head of every street" (2:19). *Oh, God, hear our prayers. Hear the cries from the people You love. Give Remy more knocks on his door.*

Our assignment was done in the buildings. However, our listening wasn't done. If our children's impressionable ears hadn't heard every "word in the book," they did so on the few blocks back. We chose not to be offended but rather to listen to the language on the street. It's not every day that we trek through this neighborhood, but it is every day that we are to hear what our culture is saying.

"Hey, there's kids right there. Hold on." Our boys heard him. A drug dealer had noticed our family. He respectfully put his drug deal on pause until we passed by. Here's what I heard in what he said: "Don't be lured by what we offer, but look at us. It's an addiction. Choose wisely."

· · · · · ·

Now you are becoming aware of the voices that matter to God's ears and are shaping the land on which you live. There's a culture to learn. There's a thing called *etiquette*, which is still very much a thing.

Every organization, church, and team has a culture and a language, whether on purpose or by accident. It's found in vision statements, shouted at practices and games, and displayed in company hallways. Our towns have a language and a culture too. It's formed by the history, the people, and their values. What is everyone talking about? What matters to your culture? What is its history?

God can't use elitists. An elitist will compare cultures—ones they lived in before, ones that existed before—and expect their current place to get on board yesterday. They grow frustrated and walk around with their hands over their ears while chanting, "That's not how you do it. We don't do it that way." Comparing cultures is dangerous. To live sent in today's world is to listen and to invite conversations with words that aren't necessarily the ones swirling around in your mind.

Listening Requires Attention

I can listen to a friend tell me all about her wine collection and not have a desire to start my own. I can hear adventurous stories of another friend's camping weekend away and be thankful I wasn't there. I can stop on the sidewalk and let those people with clipboards tell me about the petition they want me to sign. Sign me up for cleaner parks. "I think children are a gift from God, no thank you," I voice to another petitioner. I take a seat in our school auditorium and listen as classes proclaim the speeches and songs of those who stood up for minority rights. In the winter assembly, I learn about all of the holidays in December without hearing mention of Christmas. In my soul, I hear the voice of a baby in an obscure stable that echoes, "Emmanuel, God is with us."

Our communities speak what is valued, what is worshiped. Listen to the billboards. The culture cares and carries opinions. Do you hear what is being said at protests, rallies, polling places, and city hall? Listen to the young voices. The feeble voices. What is being spoken is what is being valued. To listen we need to have conversations. If you listen, you can learn, which can lead to better understanding and compassion. Listening shows we value one another. Listening paired with action matches what God's Word says when He tells us to "be doers of the word, and not hearers only" (James 1:22).

Stephanie didn't think they would be here long, maybe two to three years at most. But she and her husband fell in love with the city and decided to buy and call this place home. Their love waned shortly thereafter, as trash and unlovable neighbors dominated their surroundings. But because her faith family lived in the same square miles and provided weekly reminders that she was not alone in learning to love the people where she lived, she began to see the people on her street differently. The problems didn't go away. She continued to struggle to love the very people who made life a challenge, but she chose not to get angry at their brokenness and not to fault them. Through prayer, Stephanie gave love, for that's what they desperately needed.

Stephanie started visiting the park across the street from her house, protecting her young son from the rough activity of the school kids. As her son Patrick started toddling around, he was drawn to those kids. Rather than retreating, Stephanie approached the teachers who were out in the park during recess hours to learn about the kids' backgrounds. They described the world in which these children were living: 20 percent were homeless, and 100 percent qualified for free or reduced price lunch. Her heart broke. It was personal now. She had listened to their stories. Over time, with multiple trips to the park every week, she and Patrick got to know the kids. They expected to see Patrick at the park. As he shared a name with the caregiver of the public park, the schoolchildren began to call Stephanie's son Little Patrick and the caregiver Big Patrick. Little Patrick loved to climb onto Big Patrick's John Deere tractor in the park shed. The second graders also called Little Patrick *friend*, as they all started sharing this little plot of green space in the city. Patrick has planted more seeds than he can count on this field as he and his mom have loved well, expecting nothing in return.

Listening to the Truest Voice

Creation speaks. The Creator speaks. Heed both voices, but one is truest. If it's creation's voice, take it to the Creator.

"Mom, this kid said this about me." Go to the Creator together. Who does God say you are?

The sign reads, "You have to have *this* to matter." What does God say you need?

"My boss wants me to _____." What does the Holy Spirit say?

Ultimately, God has been speaking since the beginning of time concerning the people around you and me. He tells us, "But whoever listens to me will dwell secure and will be at ease, without dread of disaster" (Prov. 1:33). We take our culture's voice to Him. Voices He's very familiar with, because we are all His creation. He helps us discern what our part is in speaking truth and grace. "Let me hear what God the LORD will speak, for he will speak peace to his people, to his saints; but let them not turn back to folly" (Ps. 85:8).

Being attuned to your specific culture gives you the backstory and helps you connect the dots. Sit down with long-timers. Ask what life was like ten or twenty years ago. We love to hear where people went to school here and what they're doing now. Start the conversation with newcomers too. What are they saying?

Find a place on your map where you can go and listen to your city. Find a place where you can listen to the God of your city. I like the tree stump in our school garden, surrounded by wood chips and squeaky voices. These are the sounds of the generation who will lead this city next. I like the stroll down our long street, where I hear countless languages I don't understand, but I'm certain they are talking about the weather and the price of avocados these days.

DWELLER TIP

I think I have two gifts. One is social engagement. I use this on the playground as I chat with other moms. This is taking my gift and pairing with God's desire that all may know Him.

—Kim Etzel, mom and scientist

13

Compassion Stickers

It sits like a trophy upon my shelf. The golden lid is screwed tight to the clear jar. Shattered black pieces of tinted glass fill the jar, which used to house mayhaw jelly: pieces from the back-right window of our brand-new minivan. The glass had imploded upon the abrupt smash of a stick, an elbow—a madness to take the backpack lying in view on the backseat. I keep this jar near me as a reminder that brokenness is both a healer and a blessing.

The boys and I were celebrating one week of minivan ownership as we drove through our city. I let them carry on in the back with their silliness. It was Friday, and silliness was most definitely allowed. They were making discoveries of how the lights turn on and off, counting the number of cup holders, and noticing that the windows were so dark they deemed the van a spy mobile. I was amused by their imaginations, but forced my thoughts in another direction as we were getting deeper into downtown San Francisco. My dearest friends had just had their firstborn, and I was bringing them a meal. I was overjoyed to hug this momma and assure her she would get through the first three sleepless months and come through sane. I maneuvered around beer delivery trucks that had parked in the middle of active driving lanes with their flashers on. Cars started lining up to get onto the Bay Bridge pre-rush hour. My GPS lady confirmed we were getting close to our destination. Then the best thing ever happened. I scored a parallel parking spot right in front of their high-rise apartment building.

In my new world, parking lots are extinct. Parking spaces are at a premium. If I had known what was ahead of me, I might have majored in park-ology in college. It just might have given me back lost hours in my days and I could educate a city on how to arrange and manage its parking. Some other time. Some other life. Even the boys noticed the greatness. "Mom, this is an amazing spot! Our feet can actually touch the sidewalk when we get out. How did you do this?" I left their imaginations to the works of the magical spy mobile I was driving. Then again, it's always the simple things that are the utmost delights. I had that simple thing in my hand as I made my way to the sidewalk to join the kiddos. On a simple little device, I pressed the "lock" image a few times, delighted to hear the van beep back at me. And yes, I'm the type-A personality that presses it way too many times, as if it quadruple-locks the vehicle.

Three little lives growing up way too quickly walked with me into the apartment complex, where we encountered the tiniest of lives and were quickly wrapped up in this days-old wonder. The outside world did not exist at the moment. All of present life was summed up in three spunky, school-aged boys coming to a full stop to see how life begins so small. We celebrated a sleeping little one yet to be introduced to the outside world, and as adults we were okay with that. It was in the innocence of my boys to wonder why he was not walking and running to embrace the adventurous outside. We mommas talked logistics of warming up the meal. I caught her up to speed on the world's happenings, as if she were living in total isolation these days, and I gave all my leftover kisses for the day to this newborn.

I left with a full heart and the same three spunky kids. My insides were satisfied. The boys sprinted out the door, down the elevator, past the concierge, onto the sidewalk. Stop. Though their bodies were ahead of me, my mind was ahead of them.

Something was not right, but I couldn't quite place it. I knew I was walking toward our brand-new minivan at a normal speed, but it felt like a slow motion version of myself held me back. My heartbeat picked up speed but seemed to weigh my body down. I initially thought one of them had left the van door open, but quickly dismissed that theory. The delightful sound of the "locking van" beep would not have echoed on the streets if a door had been left open. I was now very close to our van. I saw the jagged hole in the window.

Nothing could stop the tears. I froze, not knowing what to do or who to call first. Cars driving along the Bay Bridge just overhead kept moving inches toward home. Street lights started to awake one by one. Dusk permeated the city skyline. And for the first time in a while, the city grew dark to my soul. *You did this to me!* is what my soul was screaming at San Francisco. *You did this! It's your fault!*

My heartbeat did not slow down. I called our friends with the newborn. They weren't answering. I called my husband, Ben. He was out of town, and that's not where I needed him to be at the moment. He spoke calmly from afar and gave me a plan. I called our friends again, and this time they answered. They came down. I called the police and filed a report over the phone. I circled the van, looking for other damages. The police officer ordered me to look into the hole. "What was taken?" she asked.

Taken? Isn't a broken window enough? I thought to myself.

My naïveté gets the best of me at times. I had everything and everyone of mine with me. The boys didn't have everything with them though. Their backpacks should have been exactly where they'd thrown them after a full week of school. They should have been lying on the van floor. Their lunch boxes should have been inside their backpacks. Leftover soggy sandwich edges and spilled raisins should have been inside that.

"Really? A kid's backpack?" My heart grew angry and hard.

People passed me on the sidewalk as if my experience was an everyday occurrence and I would get through it. Who was passing by when the crime happened? Tell me that, San Francisco! Dozens of people going to and fro, headed to happy hour or home. And I stood numb and completely shaken up by the disaster before me.

Turn around. The sliver of light in my soul not conquered by darkness nudged me. My numb self moved.

With the jagged, broken window behind me now, I saw my three boys crouched before me, tucked under the overhang of the apartment complex. They were hurting. Their backpacks had been stolen. Their spy mobile had a hole in it. Their mommy was a mess, and all they could do was cower in the corner. The real me wanted to cower with them. The real me wanted to grab them up in my arms and run as far away from the city as I could go. The real me wanted to run back to the familiar, all the way back to the Midwest or Southeast. The real me wanted to believe that brokenness was contained only in this place, and I was among it and wanted out. Instead, I promised the boys that it would be okay. I promised them what I was begging God to promise me. I held them like I was needing God to hold me. All on a sidewalk, staring into brokenness.

I mustered up the willpower to brush broken glass off the seats that the boys needed to be strapped into for the short ride home. Brand-new meant nothing. Broken meant everything. Had it just been me, I would have processed this moment entirely differently on the drive home. I would have joined the sidewalk people for happy hour. To drown my sorrows and shake my fist at an ugly moment of the week. To verbally batter and bruise someone who had stolen from me. To articulate to those beside me that my week was worse than theirs. Instead I did what anyone else would do in a dark moment with young onlookers. I told them our tomorrow had changed. We were going backpack shopping.

My kids are pretty typical, so that meant questions abounded for the rest of the evening. I robotically gave answers when I had the facts, and also said numerous times, "I don't know, sweetheart. I don't know, sweetheart. I don't know."

Lying awake at night is never a good thing. My protector was three time zones away, and my mind was spinning at warp speeds, trumping the lure of rest. I was convincing myself that the smasher of my window had followed me home. I was haunted by the city at night. I kept hearing knocks, footsteps, knee-popping sounds. My mind was playing tricks on me. The sensible me knew that this was a contained moment and that it had not poisoned my children nor my life. The sleepless me continued to wrestle through the night, fighting off fears and uncertainties.

The window smasher had damaged my theology at dusk, and I ran to hide behind what I had always thought to be true—that all people are good and that a locked door means "do not enter." I wanted to know that personal belongings are just that . . . personal. I needed to hear that privacy means something to the people with whom I share Planet Earth. Digging deeper, I was begging God to tell me that I got privileges in this life because our family had stepped out to do hard things for Him and His kingdom here in this city. I was begging God to extend more righteousness to me in the most selfish of ways. I told this God that I deserved better.

God did not conform to my thoughts that night. He prefers to be higher and greater. He must have managed to speak rest as I lay solo in my bed, because I found myself waking up hours later.

If Friday's afternoon hours had allowed for silliness, then Saturday morning was dull and lazy in comparison. The boys woke to the same world they told goodnight. Not me. My world was upside down. Cartoons and bedhead hair and LEGO play were in full morning swing. I managed to sneak outside to the scene of the crime that lingered all over my mental state from the night before. Brokenness was worse in the morning light. It had magnified to reveal fragments all over the place. Goldfish crumbs and stale French fries and Cheerios that should have eventually filled the crevices had been beaten to the punch with shattered black glass. *How on earth do I get all of this out?*

Brokenness

Brokenness had to be scooped up. I began the process with a glass jar that was handy, and started dumping shards into the trash from the jar. The minivan and our family routine needed to get back to normal. The window had to be replaced and the crevices cleaned out. I, on the other hand, would never be the same. So that jar filled to the brim with bits of broken glass continues to stir me in the most redemptive way possible.

When we encounter brokenness, often more than just one of us is affected. I remember Joseph's life and hear the familiar truth that he spoke to his sinister brothers: "Do not fear, for am I in the place of God? As for you, you meant evil against me, but God meant it for good, to bring it about that many people should be kept alive, as they are today" (Gen. 50:19–20). Joseph forgave his tormenting brothers. He saw the big picture that God was painting all along. But Joseph also put actions to his words. "Thus he comforted them and spoke kindly to them" (v. 21). As if making brokenness applicable for his own life wasn't enough, Joseph extended restoration to his offenders.

I cannot fully live and love yet reason with myself to put away this moment as if checking it off a list for experiencing urban life at its worst. If I judge the window smasher I fall short of my own desperation to be restored. If I truly have been changed, I will never check off this moment but rather let it remind me over and over that God is making all things new. In the eighteenth century, Dr. Samuel Johnson wrote, "Men more frequently require to be reminded than informed."[1] That's how God deals gently with His children. He reminds us that in our brokenness and loneliness and at our worst, we are shattered of pride and control. For it's our hurting encounters that beg for a Healer. Our open wounds bleed out for His touch. Nothing else will do. Our injuries cry before God, "I've gotten hurt," and He responds with healing in His perfect time.

Band-Aids by Another Name

When hurt happens, we instinctively want to run away or look elsewhere for medicine or a quick fix or a better place to do ministry and life. There is no place on earth where hurting is nonexistent. Maybe there are places where it seems more minimal. But truth be told, when we are living sent, we will encounter spiritual attacks from the enemy and hurt from people who don't get what we're about. Let's not act surprised when brokenness happens. Rather, let's be proactive and see it as providing opportunities to pray, do self-inventory (confession, repentance), and extend compassion.

As the Healer deals with our wounds that connect to our soul, we wear Band-Aids and distribute Band-Aids. We live life among others wearing Band-Aids—covering up hurt and pain. Band-Aids are strips of plastic tape with a patch of cloth we humans can administer. Band-Aids are compassion stickers. We don't avoid the hurting people; we become the agents by which they access the Healer. Healed people hand out compassion to hurt people. We don't let their hurt cause us to hurt back, but we apply a Band-Aid to ourselves and extend one to them. Stop the hurt. Let the healing begin.

Notice the togetherness in Jesus's parable:

The kingdom of heaven may be compared to a man who sowed good seed in his field, but while his men were sleeping, his enemy came and sowed weeds among the wheat and went away. So when the plants came up and bore grain, then the weeds appeared also. And the servants of the master of the house came and said to him, "Master, did you not sow good seed in your field? How then does it have weeds?" He said to them, "An enemy has done this." So the servants said to him, "Then do you want us to go and gather them?" But he said, "No, lest in gathering the weeds you root up the wheat along with them. *Let both grow together* until the harvest, and at harvest time I will tell the reapers, 'Gather the weeds first and bind them in bundles to be burned, but gather the wheat into my barn.'" (Matt. 13:24–30, emphasis added)

Wounded, we live together. Healed, we live together.

Band-Aids cover up the wounds, absorb the bleeding, and can be distributed as a way to help and to start a conversation. "I see your hurt. I know what that feels like. There is only one Healer. Here's what I do with my pain." We tell our story. We listen to theirs. If we live protected and isolated and have "avoid certain parts of town" lives, we don't know Jesus as the Healer and Mender of our soul.

Band-Aids are a vulnerable way to be real with our neighbor—to live life raw and authentic. When your heart breaks for what breaks God's, though, a simple Band-Aid will do. The Healer does the deep work. Band-Aids say that He's still working on me. I've gotten hurt, and I'm letting the healing take place uninterrupted. I know it doesn't feel good, and while I can't take your pain away, this Band-Aid will help. As kids, we thought that Band-Aids heal. They don't. They only protect and cover so the healing process doesn't get interrupted.

The window smasher needed Band-Aids after making off with my boys' backpacks at dusk. I would give that person a Band-Aid for the glass cuts that must be there. It's how we touch one another. How we walk through hurt together. If we don't see the hurt, we won't see the help.

In our big, small city, I have possibly encountered him (or her) on the streets unbeknownst to either of us. This person has been prayed for by me and my boys. That morning when I saw my brokenness in the glass in the backseat of our brand-new minivan, Jesus's work in me was not confined to me. It never is, if Jesus truly is at work. Cartoons and LEGO play came to a brief pause. There was nothing I could do for the bedhead hair, though. We held hands in the living room and prayed for the person who was hurting so much they had smashed a window. We prayed for the person desperate for "what could be" in a backpack. Together, we thanked God for His protection over our bodies. We prayed for this momma's heart. I needed just as much healing as the smasher did. The God of my city is the God I want to know. He sent His Son Jesus to die, and it's as if the window smasher and I are there beside Him. One to His left and one to His right. I want the window smasher in heaven as much as I want to be there. I'm done throwing stones and have moved on to compassion sticker distribution. I hope he or she is done smashing windows.

DWELLER TIP

Got an extra sofa or spare bed? Let someone crash for a night or two while they're in transit.

—Ben and Kim Chelf, entrepreneurs

it's a lifestyle

• • • • • •

Build houses and live in them; plant gardens and eat their produce. . . . But seek the welfare of the city where I have sent you into exile, and pray to the LORD on its behalf, for in its welfare you will find your welfare.

Jeremiah 29:5, 7

14

Choose to Stay

We started this walk by declaring "I can start to stay." Are you at the point of wanting to stay? Choosing to stay? Getting to stay? Do you have a few stories of God's faithfulness that are fueling your faith as you are learning to love where you live? We're halfway through our walk together. The welcome mat is out, and we're putting the essentials to use. Now it's time to make this a lifestyle.

The strategies we will unpack together are not intended to add to your already-overcrowded calendar. They are to shape that calendar and give meaning to your schedule. We'll use what we've got around us and in us to love well. We'll have fun, and we can trust that others will feel cared for and satisfied. Here's what will launch this lifestyle into a life that chooses to stay—today, or as long as God grants.

Face Reality

Everything is a work in progress, especially us humans. Our faith is also a work in progress. Our culture and towns make the list. Our homes too. You and I both know something newer, prettier, higher tech, and more ideal will come along. That's a normal part of the progression. Living sent is not getting swept away but being mindful of the direction our world is going and certain of what God's Word has to say about it.

The seasons of life bring demands that we see as either obstacles or opportunities. Embrace the progress. The point of living sent is not to arrive but to travel well in this one life we've been given. It will require we get outside—of our homes and ourselves. Realize that relationships take time and investment. As a start, read this chapter outside your home. Say you have an appointment and meet me on Main Street to discuss the real issues of life—people we get to love because He first loved us. This certainly is a process!

Be for Your City

We need to be for the places we live in all ways that aren't contrary to God's ways. Because you are a citizen of God's kingdom, you want to be the best possible citizen of _____ (fill in where you live). What will this take? For me to be for my city, I compost and recycle. I consider the options to bike, walk, or transit around town. Buying a book at the local bookstore puts food on my neighbor's table and contributes to their water bill. Citizens in my city put free stuff on the curb. And we're collectively okay with this. I've scored a beach chair, a kitchen chair, and bookshelves. I've helped another citizen load a Pottery Barn crib off a curb that she planned to take to a pregnancy care center.

In the city of Kampala, Uganda, our church partners with the United Christian Center on several levels—one of which is to provide trades and skills for the locals so they can earn a profitable income for their family. A team from our church had the honor of participating in the graduation for their cosmetology students. Upon graduation, the church leaders lined the graduates up outside the church, and we got in line behind them. The women received business cards for their new salons to hand out. But this wasn't enough celebration; coming up behind us was a marching band! We paraded through the streets, proudly cheering on their hard work and announcing they were open for business! That's being for a city and the people of the city. What does your town rally around? How can you join in?

Know Your Motives

Jesus knows my heart and your heart and his heart and her heart. He sees the motives behind our fears and behind our generosity. Why do we do good works? When done as a good gesture, they speak lovingkindness but can only go as far as humanity allows them. When done with the love of Christ, He sees them as an offering, and He has a way of multiplying those! If we act with the love of Christ, a shift happens—His kingdom comes to earth as it is in heaven. This is why we look up before we look out. This is why our action starts with prayer. Prayer aligns our motives with His.

Brace Yourself

This lifestyle is inconvenient, because "Christ-lifeness" is inconvenient when compared to worldly standards. Think about Christ and His ministry. Did He only go to towns so He could rest and be served? No! He healed. He fed. He touched people. He invited others to come alongside Him. He mourned. He ate. He engaged the religious crowd, the government officials, the outcasts. He attended weddings. He went into people's homes. He spent loads of time with his closest friends. Inconvenience, when recognized for what it is and who it's from, creates a release in the soul. Living sent will require something of you. You'll do it surrounded by imperfect people who don't understand why you're reaching out or why you came. It requires selflessness—to hold out your hands and say, "Whatever, God; have Your way." And He will, and you can.

Celebrate along the Way

Take whatever brings you joy and lead with that. Take the best parts of you and use that gift up. God amazingly will keep refilling it as you use it to bless others. This means taking what is uniquely you and gifting it to others. The celebration happens when others receive your gift, and also when they follow suit. So make it a game! For me, when I get to smile at someone and they smile back, or I say hi and they gift the word right back—that's winning in my culture. When the neighbor kid comes out to play with our kids, we're calling that success. These might be givens for you, but think of the wins in your culture. What "scores" as a deeper connection? It's a given that when people come over in my community, they come bearing chocolates, flowers, or wine. The win happens when they feel at home and verbalize that they can't wait to get together again soon.

Think of what brings you joy. Think of what brings your community joy. Then dance, sing, throw a party, and count your blessings.

Choose to Stay

Why do we do this anyway? What's the point? We are made to worship Him and lead others to do the same. If our cities and towns don't know Him, we make the introductions. They need to see how good He is, how loving and kind a Father He is. How each of us makes Him known is intertwined with our uniqueness and courage, using the essentials. God is ready to use every part of you where you live. Choose to stay—because the opportunities are about to come.

. . . . . .

I want to help you choose to stay by seeing your corner of the world in quadrants, circles, and hubs. Quadrants are geographical locations around town. Circles are groups of people we form or find ourselves in. Hubs are our homes. Are you ready to get started?

DWELLER TIP

Explore, engage, and enjoy the culture of your city. Find hidden gems and become a regular. Embrace where you are and make it yours.

—Gilbert family, still exploring New Orleans,
fourteen years and counting

15

Quadrants

Let's begin with quadrants. The concept of quadrants is to maximize impact in four physical locations. Where you call home might have the north part of town, the south, the east and west. Some towns are divided by train tracks and Main Street.

In our Missouri life, we lived and did school in one community and did church and work in the neighboring town. In our Alabama life, we lived and did preschool on the south side of the college town while doing church, work, and play in the central part of town. It's debatable as to how many neighborhoods or districts make up my home now. There's some obvious ones: Mission, Financial (FiDi), Tenderloin, Sunset, Richmond, and SoMa (South of Market). And the micro-neighborhoods: Cathedral Hill, Mission Terrace, Silver Terrace, and Sunnyside.

This is a quadrant. Notice the words in each square: *work*, *home*, *school/play*, and *church*. Each quadrant represents where you do much of life.

It's your turn. Take the following places and put them in the correct square. Are they in the vicinity of work, home, school/ play, or church?

WORK	HOME
SCHOOL/PLAY	CHURCH

Quadrants

Grocery store

Gas station

Gym

Extracurricular activities

Doctor's office

Standing appointments (hair, nails, therapy, coffee, dry cleaning, etc.)

Perhaps you're thinking of all the other places you must go in a given week, and some are nowhere near work, home, school, or church. Write those in a space outside of the squares.

· · · · · ·

The key is to make choices that overlap life as much as possible into four geographical locations in town. The idea is to simplify life, to create deeper connections. If you're driving all over town, that's complicated (unless your town only has six traffic lights). Schedule your meetings around your workplace. Host at your home. Play sports and eat ice cream near the school. Grocery shop near the church. Fill your car up with gas near work or home. Choose standing appointments in these quadrants.

The Gym in Quadrant #3

I've brought you to the gym with me. Relax. There aren't body-builders here at 8:00 a.m. All types are welcomed at this particular location. It's why I keep coming back. I want you to meet my friends. I tell Janet I want to be as active as her when I've had as many trips around the sun as she has. Lonnie loves Giants baseball; she and her husband have been listening to games for years. Did you catch that? Listening. It's a ritual they share together as she accomplishes housework while simultaneously cheering on her favorite team. My sons give me baseball updates so that I have plenty to talk about with Lonnie. Carolyn has called this neighborhood home for years. She's raised her kids, who are now raising their kids. Sam is faithful. You'll see his bike parked outside. He's got his routine down, and it's inspiring.

One day I walked up to a gal whom I vaguely remember talking to about her kids and schools. Reintroductions take courage for me. She said, "Are you a real estate agent? I feel like our paths have crossed outside of the gym."

"No, I'm not."

"You look like my friend's agent."

"No. That would be a fun job. I'm a pastor's wife."

"Yep. Nope. Our paths wouldn't have crossed there!"

But she probably *has* seen me somewhere else, because my gym is in one of my quadrants. These are my people at the gym in quadrant #3 (school/play). I feel at home in this place. I've got names and faces, and, well, they've got me. And as I listen to my music on the elliptical machine, I'm praying for them by name, for their days, their kids, and for them to discover the Life Giver. This is the quadrant where my kids go to school and play sports. It's also home to the donut shop where we celebrate on Fridays for making it through a long week. It's the quadrant where Ben does his sermon walks and where I like to treat myself to a pedicure. My friends at the salon are brilliantly bilingual (maybe more). We initially communicated through head nods and smiles. Now, Karen likes to practice her English with me, and I love to learn about her Vietnamese way of doing life. We'll wave to them when we walk by.

Benefits of Quadrants

Consider how you can scale down and live in only four areas (or less) of your city on a regular basis. Establishing quadrants early on helps establish community and rhythms. It tightens your influence but deepens it at the same time. You start seeing the same people. Relationships can go deeper more quickly.

People start recognizing you as you frequent stores, businesses, and restaurants.

Conversations get extended because you're not having to rush over to the other side of town.

You are comfortable borrowing a cup of sugar or jumper cables.

You know when festivals, block parties, games, and community events are happening.

Our complex world becomes simpler through knowing people and becoming familiar with our surroundings.

. . . . . .

Quadrants are the physical places we go. They can be found on a map. The goal is to shrink our footprints from being all over God's creation to walking our soles out in four areas or less. Would it be greater to encounter a thousand people in your town a week, coming and going, with short interactions, or to have meaningful conversations with five people you see on a regular basis?

Let's do more in less space. Rather than saving your prayers for bedtime, pray for the server at the restaurant as you thank God for the food. Find the nursing home in one of your quadrants. I guarantee they will welcome your time. We've been known to get a sleeve of quarters from the bank and feed a few parking meters in one of our quadrants. Bake cookies for the service people in your neighborhood: the postal worker, the delivery team, and the waste management department.

Do you find yourself in more than four areas of town? You're an extremely busy person. Perhaps you need to scale down. It will never be perfection, though. We have to do life outside of our quadrants occasionally. I love our orthodontist, who is out near the ocean, and our pediatrician, who is south of the city and has ample parking spaces. Quadrants are where we spend daily life. So let's try to maximize time in our quadrants. Perhaps your city has a glorious amount of libraries or parks. Pick two or three in your quadrants. What can you start doing closer to home or work or church or play?

DWELLER TIP

Become regulars at a nearby coffee shop. It will make your city seem smaller and more personal when the barista greets you by name and has your order ready to go!

—Josh and Katy

16

Circles

Circles are groups of people, and often they form themselves. Seasons of life and commonalities cause them to take shape; circles can last a lifetime or a season. Being part of a small group or volunteer group is a circle. A work team is a circle. Parenthood is a circle. Friendships are a circle. A social club is a circle. A sports team is a circle.

But we can also form circles. We don't wait for the welcome; we are the welcome. We see a need, and God leads us to rally others to meet that need. You might have been a part of a group in your last home and want to continue to grow those skills or use that passion in your new place. I gather our staff girls together to form a circle so we stay connected outside of ministry. A few of my writer friends have formed a circle, and we connect on the first of the month.

Let where you are determine what you say yes to. Then engage where you find favor, where you have receptivity to others. To do this, make sure your calendar has margin so you can give your yeses to your circles. See these circles as marked by God with purpose, as He has intentions that you might not see yet.

A Circle the Shape of a Diamond

One of my circles formed through Little League. On some land carved out of Golden Gate Park, I stood watching my three boys toss the baseball around. We had arrived early, like we often do when Ben is driving. For him, ten minutes early is right on time— a leadership principle I am striving for on this side of eternity. Often, as a new season begins, I prepare myself for the onset of parent introductions and get-to-know-you moments. Another family joined us on the field, and we all assumed we were there for the same initial team practice. With hesitation, I initiated a hello, and I learned that they're from Hawaii. Her husband's job had moved them to the city years ago. Now it was my turn to talk again. Jammed throat issues continued to be my disorder. But something weird happened when I ran past the word *church* in my talk. This petite Hawaiian mom beamed.

"We go to church too!" She was genuinely serious, and this family is now a part of our faith family. She and I have led small groups together at church. That's a circle. We've traveled the world. That's a partnership circle. We're still raising those kids of ours. That's a parenting circle. Little League is baseball to kids, but it's community for me. It has opened up doors for me to share why I live in the city and learn how others are raising their families here.

Circles within Circles

Sometimes we think our happiness is in the comfortable life. We believe that easy is satisfying, so we stick with easy. Meet Brett. He found this to be true in his Montana life. Not fully convinced what his major in college should be, he chose to save money and stay in state. Faith was a distant part of his life, and that created space for depression and discontentment. In what he would describe as a jolt of reality, he realized happiness wasn't in his college degree, a tech job, or anything he could conjure up. He made a drastic move to a new city and state, new time zone, and new culture. This lifestyle change gave him a chance to restart, but it wasn't easy. He first sought out a church home, then connected to a small group of people his age and put his gifts to work with the church production team. Circle one was established. He began an engineering job with a start-up that was all about helping people travel the world and feel like they could "belong anywhere." Circle two was established. He was in a small group and volunteer team. Circle three. He had a place to belong. In a short amount of time, he noticed that his new company had many affinity groups, including women in engineering, parents, LGBTQ, and veterans of the armed forces, but not one for Christians. Brett met with another coworker, and they started one. A circle within a circle. Easy isn't satisfying; purpose is. And Brett was stepping into his purpose as he stepped out of his own way. He is now engaging with purpose every day. He is living sent, and he knows it. Created circles or ones we step into are structures used by God to help us recognize purpose and be others-focused.

One day Brett invited me and Ben over for lunch at his company's headquarters. Our mutual friend Sherril found us in the commons eating area and described what it's like to know another believer at work—a circle within a circle. "It's such a blessing to see one another during the week at work. It reminds me we are not alone."

Jesus Formed Circles

Jesus picked the twelve disciples, and within that circle He had three closest friends, Peter, James, and John. In His adult years, He lived in this circle, traveled with this circle, and experienced highs and lows with this circle.

At times we can pick who we invite into circles. The circle of who speaks truth to us. The circle of who gets to speak into our kids. The inner circle of friendship. A mentor circle. We determine

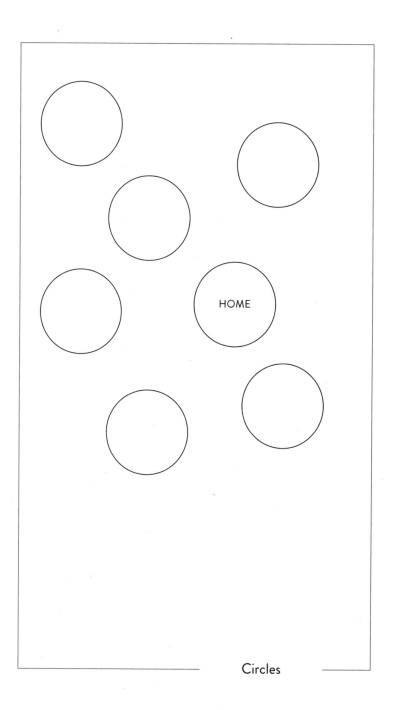

HOME

Circles

our circles on social media. They might not always be our preferred circles, but we can ask God to make known His purpose and to show us what He sees.

Jesus also mixed the circles up, and this infuriated the religious leaders. Jesus was a friend to rebels, misfits, prostitutes, tax collectors, fishermen, children, and women. His circles were always intentional. Circles are meant to blend and mix, which helps make your quadrants smaller. Tim Keller, a New York City dweller and pastor, says, "There are some needs only you can see. There are some hands only you can hold. There are some people only you can reach."[1]

Label your circles. Engage them with purpose. One of your circles will be drawn around your home—the hub.

DWELLER TIP

Enjoy eating at new restaurants? Hiking? Drinking great coffee? Invite others in to enjoy your passions and use your passions to connect with people you might not otherwise.

—Margaret and Cory, young tech professionals

17

Hubs

A hub is an effective center of a region. Think of a circle with a few spokes coming out from it. The circle is your home. The spokes are those who live near you being connected to your home. With home as a hub, it is the place where people can find us.

Make Your Home the Hub

Put your surname in the circle. The goal is to add the names of people you've met who live around you, know where you live, and recognize your home as the hub.

The guy who waves as he passes by while out on a run is not on my hub map yet. Fred is. He saw us throwing the Frisbee while he was enjoying a smoke outside. We made the introductions, and he knew where we lived. He's lived on our street for fourteen years. I told him that if he needed anything not to hesitate to come over. I identified our home as the hub without saying so. Now we look for Fred outside so we can stay connected. With home as the hub, just like our circles, we don't wait for the welcome; we are the welcome.

Hubs

Home is first and foremost a refuge within—a place where you feel safe and belong despite outside circumstances and pressures. Home is secondarily a place of blessing—a place to be opened up and spilled out for those who literally live right beside you.

This comes with challenges. Living sent opens us up to being vulnerable with others, yet gives our community the opportunity to watch how to walk through hard times rather than looking elsewhere. We get to be the ones living radical, Jesus-inspired, generous lives. Build the hub and let the spokes of those who live right beside you point toward you.

Sewage water flooded homes two blocks from us several years ago. This caused loss of possessions and weeks of cleanup. Our neighbors had to take time off of work and spend countless hours with the city to see this issue resolved and handled correctly. It can be paralyzing to know how to respond. We weren't close enough to step inside and help them sort through their possessions, but we were close enough to bring them a meal so they could take a break and not have to worry about what to eat. Focaccia and soup and chocolates from Trader Joe's were our offerings.

Here's how to know you've become the hub: if you were to leave, you'd be missed. The spokes would lose their connecter in the neighborhood. Yet hubs are reproducible. Having more than one hub gives more stability and provides a stronger safety net. Model this well and lead others to host and connect and share the load. Not everyone will step inside your home, but make it the aim that everyone knows where your home is. A day might come when they knock on your door.

Make the Hub Lo-Action

Lo-action is a shuffling of the letters in *location*. Our locations are our homes that we make the hub. I don't suppose that God ever intended for them to be staged for magazine covers but opened and used to bless others in ordinary ways. And home is one location we can practice hospitality. Not overthink hospitality. It's not just for the stay-at-home mom, the empty nester, the retiree, the immaculate homeowner, or the person attempting to write a book on such matters. It's for you, pastors and leaders and busy people. Jen Hatmaker says it this way: "Our soul aches for real people in real homes with real kids and real lives." She goes on to say not to fear humanity, for it is your best offering, and your hottest commodity is your time. So give it away and create margin to do so if necessary.[1]

This margin requires time and creates space. And for us, it necessitated pizza.

Pizza Works Wonders

My original plan seemed brilliant and well-thought-out. I would utilize everyone's gifts in the family to make our neighborhood grill night inviting and satisfying. Ben would grill the meat. Elijah would sauté the veggies. Sam would create the environment. Kavita would design the signs. Asher would greet everyone. I would set up, clean up, and be the whispering cheerleader encouraging my tribe to say hello and learn names.

Until the grill broke. I can get easily frustrated when my original plan fails, but I'm learning to embrace plan B—which is often God's plan A all along. It just takes me longer to get there.

Plan B was to get pizza and offer it to our neighbors as they came home from work. Pizza, bottled water, and cookies for free. We made large fluorescent signs and hung them on our fence two days prior. There are no other signs to read on the way to work, so this would surely get their attention. We would be ready before 5:00 p.m. and would do whatever it took to start the introductions with the people who share our sidewalks.

Where we live is a popular route to one of the city's main transit stations. Our city embraces Costco pizza for the obvious reasons. It's good and cheap and feeds an army. Everyone is comfortable with Costco pizza. We picked up ten boxes with twelve slices in each. Ben and I were either exhibiting big faith or content with a massive amount of leftovers. Perhaps both. When I picked up the pizza, the Costco guy asked what this was all for.

"We're feeding our neighborhood!"

He replied, "I wish I lived there!"

I didn't say it, but I felt it deep, *Yeah, you do!*

I really wanted everyone to step into our backyard. Not for aesthetic reasons. Heavens, no! It's a slab of concrete with some chairs. I wanted it to feel like a get-together, not a come-and-go. But Sam, using his gifts, persuaded me to move the setting from our backyard to our fence, along the sidewalk. While I wanted everyone to step inside our yard, the sidewalk was better neutral ground. Card table and us. It proved to be genius.

So, what happened? We knew people would walk by. But would they stop? They did. They wanted to pay. They wanted to know the *catch*. They couldn't believe we'd do this for free and with no strings attached. They hung around. They met other neighbors. Traffic slowed down on a rather busy street. This busy street has no shoulder, yet an ambulance, a police car, and a general contractor's truck all pulled over to get pizza! People on the bus stared. A dozen or so people we knew stopped by. But it was the forty or more strangers who wowed us! People who didn't look like us or believe like us but who walked by us and lived by us. Two deaf guys. A lesbian couple. An older lady who helped at the Jewish Community Center. A family from Costa Rica who just moved here. A family with a Down syndrome son. A single mom who also took a piece home to her daughter. Most of the neighbors had to walk across the street as we motioned them over for free pizza. If they refused, they did so with a smile. Some had to remove their earbuds. We were so proud of them. This lasted about two hours. The crowd dwindled and the wind picked up. We closed up shop.

We took our last two boxes to neighbors we knew. Asher rang the doorbell, and the lady who answered the door replied, "We didn't order pizza!"

Asher said, "We aren't delivering. We're giving it to you!"

Our pizza night helped us learn names and share ours. Neighbors shared their stories of living and growing up here. We told them we did this to get to know their names—to cause them to stop and talk. Many stuck around to learn each other's names too. We didn't mention the name of Jesus, but His presence was all around us.

I'm convinced that, the next day, as they walked by our house, they remembered pizza. But my hope is that we would become the hub. We want to be those neighbors, that family! We want to create safety in a community.

We'll do it again soon. They'll be invited to our Cookies and Cocoa in December. I'm convinced of this; it's not up to them. It's up to us. And if God can do something radical with five loaves and two fish, I can only dream what He's doing with ten boxes of Costco pizza through our tribe of six.

Personality Shapes Hubs

Home will shine when you are content in the season of life you're in. I can promise you that my parents' home now is nothing like it was when I and my sisters were growing up. Perhaps you are in a season of college students living at home or wedding planning, or an older parent has moved in, or toys are evident in every room. Let it all shine. Your small business orders are stacked for shipment in the foyer. Soccer cleats clog the back door. Home is who you are and what you can offer in the season of life you are in. It can always be a hub.

We host Cookies and Cocoa every December as a gift to our neighbors. Such a simple festive night accomplishes quite a lot. From our Christmas tree to the manger on display, our neighbors see that we celebrate Christmas. Loving our neighbor is not just an adult thing but a family affair. While our home might be perceived as warm and inviting, we know it's God's love and presence that we invited in beforehand. We strive for unity and friendship on our block.[2]

What if no one comes? This is why I host Cookies and Cocoa at the beginning of December. If no one comes, we turn the sign over, and it now reads, "Pack a Christmas Tin for a Friend." I keep a few tins stashed for this reason. We load up tins with cookies and gift them to others. I write from personal experience here. No one showed up for our Easter egg hunt. Six people showed up for our ice cream social, and one year we had a fine representation of homes for Cookies and Cocoa. We create the hub to be the welcome. If those who live near us are to know we are Christians by our love, it must be on display.

Get each other's mail when out of town. Water plants. Care for pets. When we moved into our current home, our neighbors wanted a better fence. We split the cost 50/50. That gave us tremendous favor. Now they hand us plums and apricots over the fence and we hand them clothes to mend and hem. Ms. Pam used to go through our recycling bin every Wednesday to collect bottles and cans. Now we set them out for her. She tells us, "You nice." I tell her, "And you're beautiful." Love goes both ways.

Hospitality Creates Hubs

Ben and I were invited over to Nicky and Sila Lee's home while on sabbatical in London. They had just returned home from their church-wide camp, investing in their own people, and were days away from family vacation.

They don't have time for us, I thought. I could picture their suitcases in the hallway and mounds of laundry, an empty refrigerator and a bare pantry. I imagined a grocery list and a vacation packing list on their desk. If I was right, I didn't know it.

After a round of hugs, they escorted us through the back door and into the kitchen. Nicky prepared coffee for us—cappuccinos, his specialty. I saw family pictures. Many smiles and destinations and clusters of happy people. We didn't stay in the kitchen long. They led us to the garden under the mature vines. The four of us munched on berries and sipped our cappuccinos in the early morning sun.

We leaned in and asked to hear their stories of meeting one another, stepping into church leadership, and raising a family in London. Nicky and Sila brought to life the art of using their current season of life to encourage and challenge us. They shared wisdom on parenting and marriage and didn't hold back their struggles and lessons learned. They were normal people on the other side of the pond putting our anxious minds at ease. All because they opened up their home as a place to present hospitality.

The sun seemed to break through the foliage at that moment, shedding light on such a significant time of encouragement in the garden. Ben and I know we are just two of many recipients of their hospitality. Nicky and Sila dispelled the myth that you have to be older, own your home, and have kids out of the house and more time on your hands to invite others in. Hospitality is woven into the fabric of their lives. It's not a date on the calendar; it is a daily gesture of Christ.

．．．．．．

Dwellers of faith are to practice hospitality (Rom. 12:13) to anyone in need. This opens the door for God to be honored, for His people to be taken care of, and for us to fulfill the Scriptures.

Hospitality is a universal practice that translates into any language. On our visit to Kampala, Uganda, Saddam's mom stood at the house entrance waiting for us. To see her as we got closer spoke hospitality. She offered us plantains and the best seats in the house. She listened. It was her son that we sponsored through Compassion International.

We traveled north of Africa into Europe, where the temperature was near perfection. Adi planned to grill rather than warm up the inside of their home. Flori brought out seasonal vegetables, and we ate on the patio in Oradea, Romania. He taught us to mix Fanta Orange and Coca-Cola. It's tasty. God was on the patio with us.

And He's right around the corner. While I can't recount all the meals at our friends the McCords' home, I can picture the big red bowl that always holds the salad and the offer of coffee as the night goes on. We can replicate what we discover at their home into our home. This multiplies hospitality.

My mom had a guestbook. It would magically appear as our friends were getting ready to leave, and she was insistent on them signing their names, the date, and where they were visiting from. Years later, a tornado wreaked havoc on the family home and most of our possessions were lost or ruined. Including that guestbook. Yet I can't envision my childhood yard and not think of Pastor Larry playing baseball with us. Ms. Dora and Ms. Marie were two widows who would spend Christmas with us. It's not what's in the guestbook but in our memories of the homes we have been in that is important. What do you love about the homes that have been warm and inviting to you?

DWELLER TIP

Make a list of who you want to have over to your home. Colleagues, kids' classmates, neighbors. As weekends are free, invite them over one by one.

—Ernie and Carla, lawyer and marketing strategist

18

The Sacred Field

If I waited to write all the stories until after I "got it," I wouldn't be around to write them. A journey of living sent is one in the process, and I'm most definitely still in the process. On my particular journey, a season on the field is where one of my circles has formed. A field where I have felt out of place and out of sorts. I know I'm not alone. This is common ground for all of us: sitting here and wanting to be over there. Taking one for the team.

Name that place where you don't want to be but where you find yourself standing. Let's call it the sacred field. How do we make the most of it—and better than that, how do we allow God to refine us and use us in this place?

The Greener Field

Our finite minds see greener pastures elsewhere. Our comparative mindset sees others doing elaborate and glamorous things in the other lanes of the kingdom race. We look around and know too much. Or we know too little. We're outsiders. We don't belong. We see a circle that won't let us in and a hub with no spokes. Our town seems too small to have quadrants or too large to scale down.

God wants to teach us something on the sacred field that we won't learn anywhere else. The sacred field is filled with people you won't find just anywhere. It's okay to say, "Hey, God, I'm glad You're here. Looks like it's just me and You. I need You to help me push through the awkward and hard and meet the people. I need the courage and contentment to stay rather than run." Sometimes that field is a place our flesh doesn't want to be, and it doesn't feel right—but God has put us there on purpose.

I connected with God in a place that seemed the furthest from Him. I thought I was separating the secular from the spiritual by being on a field rather than a sanctuary. He surprised me. God showed up on a field where I least expected to encounter Him, and it was sacred ground.

· · · · · ·

Where I live, games are played on Sundays. Not all of them, but lots of them. The parks are at their peak happiness then. Ragamuffin baseball fields are scattered throughout the forty-nine square miles of the city. I like clean and neat, but as the city grows on me, I appreciate these nonmanicured plots of ground that invite the small population of kids to come and play. In our first year of Little League, I thought God punished us for doing something so secular on Sundays. In my childhood culture, only sinners played ball on Sunday. My theology told me that God was only in church that one day, and if you knew God, you'd be in church too. Not at the lake or the baseball field or at home cutting grass. *God's not happy with this.* My soul played this broken record again and again.

All three boys played on three different levels at three different times at three different fields on three different days, including Sunday, with three other days for practices. It always took me a few weeks to let the reality soak in that I would be at forty-five games between March and May. Yet that reality only affected my outer façade; inside, I wrestled with it for the entire season.

On the Enneagram, a model of nine personality types, I am a perfectionist married to a performer. We like to get things done yesterday. You can imagine the calendaring to be a bit overwhelming for this one-car family—also considering one parent has his biggest workday on Sunday.

A battle waged within my aggravated spirit. My whole being had been wired to get up and put on Sunday best for thirty-plus years. My neat and organized calendar looked best with church being the only event on Sunday. Now it was crowded; now I wore tennis shoes. My pastor husband knew where he would be and joyfully let me know the afternoon games he could make. I knew where I would be and bitterly let him know all the morning services I would not attend. My heart was torn between two places. I wanted to cheer on my baseball players. I wanted to cheer on my pastor husband. Selfishly, I wanted to be with my faith family. Selflessly, I set up my camping chair down the third base line.

Not really. I was full of self, and it would be God who revealed this to me on the field.

I returned to this place every spring. I'd tell myself I was getting better at it. Ben would give you the honest answer.

"Get someone else to take the boys. Drop them off and come to church," he'd suggest.

I'd shake my head, and my insides would twist and turn. "No, of course not."

He'd tell me all that was taking place on that Sunday. A family dedication, a baptism, the announcements, a celebration. That's where I wanted to be—not on a place of dirt and grass. That broken record played on repeat.

What Happens on the Sacred Field

My theology once said that God displays His greatest grace in African huts and town ghettos. My belief in God tied Him to a location. Now I was finding God on the sidewalk. I was finding

Him on a field. He was pointing out His truth on a crowded light rail train. He was shining through my oldest cheering on his brother as he pitched the ball nervously. If God had a camping chair, He'd have it stationed down the third base line. That's where half of His children were on Sundays in the city.

I'm sure Mary had thoughts of being somewhere else delivering her firstborn than in a barn full of animals. Jonah wasn't a fan of one sacred field, so as he ran away he landed in the belly of a whale, another kind of sacred field. Sarah wanted Hagar's womb over her barren one. Heavens, Jesus wanted to be somewhere other than Calvary's cross. Yet He cried, before He got there, "Not My will, but Yours, Father."

"Isn't there another way, another place, some other time?" I ask.

This is God's answer, as best as I understand it: *No, my child. I get two for the price of one this way. You and the kids take Me to the field, and I'm refining you in the process.*

It's human to want to be somewhere else. Our struggles and desires aren't hidden from God. But His ways and thoughts are higher than ours, so we trust Him. He knows better. He sees further. He wants to teach us and shape us on the sacred field.

My prayer in the minivan driving down Sloat Boulevard to a ragamuffin ball field in one of the coldest parts of the city goes a little like this: "God, You are just as present with us on the baseball field as You are in the church." I hold out my hands at the red light. "Whatever, God; have your way."

· · · · · ·

The chain-link fence separates me from my ballplayers. Baseballs sound as they pop into gloves. Parents dress for winter and hug their thermoses of warm beverages. I push through the awkward. I extend my hand. We share names and city stories. I'm in a circle. I'm on the sacred field. Meet Coach Adam. He and his son, David, have played years of ball with us and are now connected to our faith family. The same is true for Coach Jim and his family.

Here comes Coach Ben now. He'll step into the dugout having just preached several times. Not everyone on the sacred field knows his vocation, but they know his commitment to the team, and God is using that to write more stories. Stories we would have forfeited if God only lived at church.

DWELLER TIP

Apartments for the elderly are one hundred yards from our home. We started the introductions, baked a cake, and invited them over for two hours on a Saturday afternoon. We now cohost this six times a year! It's the only time some of them get outside, and we learn so much from these elderly wise people. We even discovered that one of them used to attend school in our house in the days when it was a small private primary school!

—Nico and Carolyn Chart, Southampton, England

19

Strategic Family

My generation has to recall our childhood through our memories. We don't have pictures of everything we ate or access to comparison accounts of what our friends were doing all the time. We rode bikes on the dirt road and spent the summer in our next door neighbor's pool. I lived in a boy-dominated neighborhood. The few of us girls had cooties, and we were fine with that diagnosis. We chose to be quarantined to our trampoline or the woods behind the house. We were the untouchables—except when we had to carpool in the mornings to school. It was our parents' idea. We used the lines in the seats to determine force fields. It worked. They never got our cooties, and we thrived as a band of girls. Our family holidays involved a four-hour drive to visit grandparents. My extended family had a vacation spot we went to every single summer. We could buy the basics within our city limits, but anything beyond that required a thirty-minute drive to a bigger town.

My childhood looks drastically different from the children's in my current hood. This is how one of my boys describes his childhood: "I ride a train to church. I cheer on the Giants and the

Warriors. I play on the sidewalk and walk to the playground. When grandparents come to see me, they come by plane. I get to go to the same vacation spot my mom went to growing up."

I had a rural childhood. He's got an urban childhood. But did you notice something that was the same? That vacation spot. I like to think we have other similarities, as Ben and I try to do things with our kids that our parents did with us. These are pieces of my childhood I can gift to our children.

They also have pieces of their childhood they want to gift us. But we can't have our eyes looking back to our childhood while they are trying to show us theirs. We have to see their childhood. Even if you're raising kids in your childhood town or in a similar culture, the world is not the same as it once was, and neither are the influences and pressures. They will see things differently than you and process the culture through different eyes. Enter this lifestyle holding hands with one another, dreaming and taking risks together.

Hold Hands Together

Holding hands allows you to know who your kids are influencing and being influenced by. We don't need their permission, but we do need their perspective. Holding hands is coming alongside your kids for the sake of being present. It's a principle that says they matter. That you are doing this life together, even if you are at different places throughout the day. This is what we teach as we do life holding hands: "Hear, O Israel: The LORD our God, the LORD is one. You shall love the LORD your God with all your heart and with all your soul and with all your might" (Deut. 6:4–5). It's not a new principle. God was establishing the people of Israel in a new place. He was giving them boundaries and the greatest commandment to be passed down to the next generation.

Like the Israelites, teach God's ways "diligently to your children, and [you] shall talk of them when you sit in your house, and when you walk by the way, and when you lie down, and when you rise" (v. 7). The kids get to have "walk along the road" conversations with us that shape how they see the world and what part in it they want to play. What do you get to do where you live? These conversations happen while we're out and about. They happen as we engage and interact with our community. Let them see and engage the hurting world in an age-appropriate way. Rewrap and sell baseball cards for money to help build a well. Pack a goodie bag for teachers. Prayer walk around the school. Teach the essentials to your kids—how to walk, how to see, how to listen, how to give compassion. If you are living sent beside them, the Holy Spirit is the Great Translator. He can take your heart and replicate it.

Busyness is not the exception today but the norm, and it often interferes with a handholding lifestyle. We have to think strategically and then follow through, or our intentions of raising a family of purpose will not happen. Let's not be choppy families but cohesive families. While we live with the "divide and conquer" approach as we maneuver around town and into classrooms and sporting arenas, we leave margin for togetherness that is seen and unseen. We eat most dinners together as a family around our table. If life feels like one is here and the other is there and you're passing each other at the front door of your home, then no one needs to tell you that your family life is choppy. This squelches the strategic family. When the kids are young, the family seems more cohesive, as they can't really be without you, but as they get older, we have to protect the calendar and our time together. Even though kids gain more freedom and are given more responsibilities, they need handholding more than ever. Hold hands as you pray for your meals. Hold hands as you speak a blessing over them at night. Grab their hand and give it a squeeze as they exit your car or leave the house for the day.

Live your faith in front of them. Let them see you struggle in decision making at work. Let them see you serve your spouse. Tell them what God is doing in your life. This will happen as you hold hands, as you discuss the day around the table, as you pray together. Ben prays this over our family: "Make us a family of dreamers—pursuing and believing You, the God of the impossible."

Inside the figure, write out a prayer for your family. Write ways you will hold hands together. A strategic family treats home as headquarters, the city as a playground, and the church as extended family.

Home as Headquarters

In our home, we teach our kids that there is God's way and humanity's way. If we choose God's way, there is blessing in obedience. If we choose humanity's way, then we step outside of the protection of God. As we intentionally make God central in our home, our kids come to understand a value system and a worldview that honors people and upholds love, justice, grace, and truth. Culture influences, but culture doesn't control. Kids influence, but kids don't control. It's at home that this is learned. This is not a helicopter parenting approach. It's walking alongside, seeing the world together, being fully present, and being their teacher, helper, and support.

A strategic family raises godly kids, not safe kids. This family sees purpose beyond the home and into the church and the city. We set up systems at home for the purpose of stability when friendships and culture aren't always stable. Culture can bite. Our enemy darts around, bruising and dinging our outer layers. We pull together and give each other the best support we can—we pray as a family for the smallest and biggest things on the planet. It's what binds us.

Systems are methods and practices that work for you but might not necessarily be beneficial for everyone. But the purpose of each system is still the same: to bring stability for the good of the family. Put God at the center of decisions, your day, your planning, your

Ways your family will hold hands together.

marriage, and your career. Then unleash creativity, which God gives us to explore, shape, build, invest, you name it.

Here are a few of the Pilgreen systems that work for us.

Every Thursday is picnic night at home. We lay out the picnic blanket in the living room, and I throw together some finger foods as we throw aside some table manners to laugh and unwind after a busy few days. Picnic night is an expected part of the week. In a gingham-patterned-picnic way, it unites us.

Every morning we pray on the way to school. Each kid shares one thing at the forefront of their mind. In other words, what they are thinking about the most on the way to school. It's typically a kid who's been absent, a test, or a field trip happening that day. Sometimes it includes a bully, a lost jacket, or a runny nose. We give it all to Jesus before we enter the schoolyard.

Plastered on our kids' bedroom walls are the names of their classmates. At bedtime, the kids choose a name or two. We pray that these classmates will sleep well, eat well, and be loved well. We pray we will be a truthful friend to them. It's at these times when we get more raw information as our children are still and contained to a mattress.

We display to the culture and each other that we're a family, and that means something. This means our answers are similar. Not the same, but similar. We have somewhere to be on Sundays. We avoid certain TV shows because of what they do to our attitudes. At school, the kids have their own identities and personalities that shine, but when it comes to our contribution and influence, they know we are the Pilgreen family. We're going to make the teachers' days brighter and make sure their classmates have pencils, snacks, and prayer support if there's a need. We guard family nights at home and want our kids to believe that the happiest place in the world is being together as a family.

Your Playground, Your Campus

See your city limits as the family playground and campus. For where you live is your children's childhood. Try a different restaurant from your usual ones. Take a front-row seat to the history, science, technology, and the arts. Build up the immunities and get outside! Explore where you live together. We've discovered that our city has windmills, roaming bison, goats that cut grass, museums with free days, and a fortune cookie factory.

But there will be obstacles, and these seem magnified with children. Choose to see them as adventures. This is what builds character in you and your kids. Our family has seen broken glass, broken people, and protests. Our cities and towns afford us adventure with life lessons. See them as such.

Let God use the people, the culture, and the surroundings to shape their thinking. Yes, God uses all of these for His glory and purpose. As you walk along the way, see what piques their interest and surrender those things to God. Rather than us pushing our childhood or what we want them to be when they grow up upon them, we need to give our kids space to hone in on what's around them and what they're exposed to. It could be that the homelessness issue propels them toward politics or social justice. Or the trains that go by steer them toward engineering.

Church as Extended Family

The church also functions as a family. Outside of the home, it's church people who understand you the most. They are doing life with you in the same culture. Invite these voices into your family DNA. Give them permission to speak into your children, and provide opportunities for your family to speak into those older and younger. The McCord kids used to entertain our kids, and now ours are the older ones entertaining the younger ones. Church is a great place for them to practice adult interaction as well.

The connections of church as extended family can be long-lasting and span generations. Though Jane Jacobs doesn't reference church here, her comments are fitting:

> Two parents, to say nothing of one, cannot possibly satisfy all the needs of a family-household. A community is needed as well, for raising children, and also to keep adults reasonably sane and cheerful. A community is a complex organism with complicated resources that grow gradually and organically.[1]

Where does your faith family gather? Is it accessible and welcoming? Where can you gather and model family with arms wide open? We need to be seen together in the community for those who've yet to step inside.

What's spoken at headquarters is confirmed at church. God is good and true. He loves us. He has a plan. This adds stability to the strategic family. What's then taught at church is reinforced at headquarters. Our kids' foundation can be doubly secure with headquarters and church working together.

Reach a Generation

John wrote, "I have no greater joy than to hear that my children are walking in the truth" (3 John 4). The God who called you here is not a God who leaves you and your family at the front door of a new place. No! He's moved in with you and has already prepared the way for you and your family here. His ways are higher, and He sees what still remains unseen to us. Satan wants to take any insecurities and turn them into lies. All the more, remember who you are and whose hands you're holding. Christ defines you. Not the city or the job or the school. God wants to see you thrive here. Be comforted in knowing God is holding your hand. Your town is watching. The people notice how you raise your kids and love your spouse. Our God is watching and is raising up families to demonstrate His grace and His truth.

A strategic family raises a generation, not just a child. We have four kids in our family. If we take our quadrants and circles and multiply by the six of us, we can really make an impact. This is discipleship at its core. Let's live this well. In my city and at this moment, it is highly possible to reach an entire people group: the children of San Francisco. But we need strategic families here. We need believers awake, brave, and involved. I'm seeing families that are getting to know their neighborhoods and building better programs at their schools. The climate is changing. Now's not the time to bail on your city but to be the people, the families, who make it better, more stable, and more grounded in the truth of Jesus Christ. What impact can your family have?

DWELLER TIP

Anyone can engage in a conversation or smile politely once. It's with the second smile and follow-up conversations that meaningful relationships begin to grow and new faces become familiar. If you have children, encourage them to initiate conversations with the people they frequently see too! It teaches them initiation, confidence, and, most importantly, to acknowledge all beings.

—The Williams, a military family

20

Position Matters

We often live where we live because we work where we work. How we are positioned in our community can be a tremendous blessing if we see the purpose in our jobs. We'll need to think bigger. Think wider. Think creatively. Be open to how God will use us because of our position. While we can be inspired from others' stories, the best way to leverage our position is by tapping into *our* gifts, wiring, and resources. That's what God wants to use. He positions us to make Him visible and accessible. And all of His positions are crucial because people's lives are at stake.

Brenda, who speaks English as a second language, can reach a people.

Hal, a truck driver, will reach a certain people.

Titin, a chemist, will reach a particular group.

Stan, a dentist, will reach a number of clients.

Jill, a barista, will reach a certain people.

Author and educator Parker J. Palmer says,

When we live in this close-knit eco-system called community, everyone follows and everyone leads. Everyone who draws breath "takes the lead" many times a day. We lead with actions that range from a smile to a frown; with words that range from blessing to curse; with decisions that range from faithful to fearful.[1]

He continues, "I am responsible for my impact on the world whether I acknowledge it or not. . . . And if I may say so, so are you."[2]

Some friends of mine want to show you how they are leading from their positions. Eugenia has invited us along to a networking event. We'll see Julia at the parade and Darren and Darrell downtown. You will notice that their "duties varied, but their commission [was] one."[3] My friends here have varied positions in the city, yet they all see their placement as being from God, to do greater works than what is temporary.

Partnering with God

Eugenia is the graceful, confident one over there with several colleagues and clients around her. She might be a tax partner at one of the largest accounting firms in the world, but she operates out of another position that fuels her conversations, business dealings, and relationships.

The path Eugenia took to her current position wasn't clear or formulated. Beginning with her childhood, she knew her family was positioned by God. Her parents were missionaries and lived day by day trusting God to meet their basic needs. She learned to ask God for anything and everything, knowing He hears her prayers and has unlimited resources.

With needing God to show up as her way of life, Eugenia questioned her calling into the corporate world where a salary would meet those needs. Taking everyone else out of the equation and fixing her eyes on God, she was certain He had His hand in this and that she was to change her college major to accounting. Eugenia's parents encouraged her to step into what God was calling her to do. She knew that her position as an accountant served a purpose no different than her parents' position as missionaries: to point others to Christ.

The God of her childhood was the God of her college days, and the same faithful God walked with her into a position as first-year accounting staff. When her colleagues asked about her weekend plans, she would mention church. If the company had a Bible study group, she joined it, and if there wasn't one, she would gather with others who were interested in starting one. Her staff began to ask how she dealt with stress in such a calm manner.

"Do you want the real story or the PC [politically correct] version?" she would ask.

Many would ask for the real story, and Eugenia would then share her faith—for it's the truest part of her. Working her way toward becoming a partner didn't change her position with God. Her career has taken her around the world. God has given her favor as she has made Him known in small circles around the office, around dinner tables, and at networking events.

In the mingling that occurs before such company events, Eugenia is in tune with the Spirit's direction and is not afraid to ask questions. It doesn't take her long to get to the topic of faith as people share their pasts, beliefs, or ambitions. Even parents of young professionals will ask her to look after their adult children who have recently joined her company or become clients.

It was at one of these events that Eugenia chatted with a young Asian lady, Cathy, about faith. And another young Asian lady. Then another. Eugenia speaks Mandarin, and it's such a comfort to these young professionals to find someone in the network welcoming them into her life. Eugenia began by meeting with these girls individually, then arranged for them to start meeting all together.

This group eventually grew to twenty-five ladies and met for over four years.

Cathy's faith, which took root in Beijing, grew as she met with Eugenia. She continued to share her faith with her parents back in China, wanting them to know God. Twelve years later, they wanted this truth for their lives. They flew to San Francisco and were baptized the same day as Cathy! I vividly remember her father coming up out of the water with his fists raised high in the air.

Five of these ladies have been baptized since they came into Eugenia's life. They know her as a partner in the largest accounting firm in the world, but more than that, they know her as a sister in Christ. She has been positioned to be a blessing. And Eugenia doesn't slow down. She recently showed me a picture on her phone of a glued-cotton-ball sheep with a Scripture written at the bottom of the page that had been created by a little boy at church. This little boy belonged to one of the ladies she had mentored who now lived across the Bay Bridge. Her influence is far reaching, and yet she's never had to go one step farther than where God has wanted her to go.

"As long as God knows my intentions, He's the One I answer to," she said.

Eugenia likes the partnership she has with her heavenly Father, for He's the only One who knows the exact number of people she's reaching, though she's doing her part to touch as many as she can here on earth.

A Civic Champion

Julia blends into the parade of colors walking through the Italian neighborhood. She's holding a flag in one hand, and her other hand is waving at us. She has the gift of noticing what's all around her, championing the beauty of the people and the place. Her smile says how honored and overjoyed she is to be a part of this city. She is there representing a large civic organization as its president. Over time, and in very precious conversations, Julia explains to others that her good works come from a well that doesn't run dry. Her influence and respect grow as others become acquainted with her faith in God. Her position in this organization might take her all over the city, but those she serves one-on-one are never taken out of her heart. She is the hands of Christ to the marginalized and the businesspeople—all because of how she sees her position.

The Gatekeeper

Darrell ran from home, from an abusive marriage and all the family she knew. She found shelter with a friend until she could get a job and live on her own. She started as the receptionist of a large financial institution in San Francisco and moved around in the company before reaching a position responsible for overseeing 167 advisors.

Darrell grew up going to church and "working for the Lord." God was out there for her to please, not inside for her to know. Working with so many people who would fire harshness at her, she would fire the same back at them. It was the difficult reality of the corporate world in which she worked. Now she sees that God has placed her back as a receptionist. "The gatekeeper," she is called.

Darrell found a church. She realized that the God she had been working for didn't need to be defended but rather befriended. She took on His life as she gave up her will and her ways. She began to see that God wanted every part of her and wanted to be everywhere she was—including the front desk. Her Bible went with her. This book was a tangible reminder that she wasn't alone. It had a place on her desk, and she would often read during the workday.

Hundreds of people walked by this gatekeeper, and one of them was Darren. When his mom, who lived in Los Angeles, was diagnosed with cancer, he returned to church. He needed somewhere to put his energy since he was far from home. His mom, who was fighting for her own life, was also praying diligently for her son. He began to see that God was positioning him in the city, in the church, in the corporate world, and in Christ alone. She's healthy again and the cancer is gone from her body, but she will never be the same. Neither will Darren.

As he followed the ways of Christ, his perspective changed. God wasn't contained in the church but was also in the financial institutions. God was present during meetings and business transactions.

One day Darren opened the office door and walked toward the front desk like he had done for years. But he noticed something new this time.

"That's a pretty good book," Darren said to Darrell, the receptionist.

"You've got that right!" Darrell now waited for these kinds of conversation starters, because her position had purpose.

To Darren, this identified Darrell as a Christian. A religious person might wear a cross, but a religious person wouldn't display her Bible, hoping to share her faith.

"Darrell is that reminder of God's presence for me," he said. "She has so much knowledge and could work anywhere, yet she's positioned as the gatekeeper to our company."

Darren and Darrell have begun to identify other Christ-followers in the company. Though Darrell was eventually asked to put her Bible away (good thing His Word can be found online!), Darren gave her some devotional books, which could stay visible and still become conversation starters. Clients and brokers would notice the books and asked her what she was reading. Some even asked if she would read the day's devotional to them. These two find such joy in conversations in their company that lead to Jesus. Darrell can see no other way now. She might know how much more money those in "higher" positions make, but she sits at the gate with the greatest knowledge in the world. She's just waiting for someone to ask.

Passion in Position

I can feel inferior in my position when I chat with friends in grander roles, yet the reality, the live-sent lifestyle, is when we see our placement as God positioning us with the ultimate goal of pointing others to Jesus. We are not to lord over others but to love others because of the Lord. When Jesus is our commonality, we have significant conversations together despite where we work in society. When we speak of Jesus, we have something in common, no matter if we are the person at the front desk, the one in the global office, the one leading the nonprofit, or the one in the classroom.

We share with one another—not just our budgets, number of conference attendees, or net sales this month but who we demonstrated generosity and kindness to, and who now knows that Jesus is the best thing about our life.

How do we do this? We take what God gives us and use it all up.

Have an extra home or guest bedroom? Say to another, "come and refresh."

Company buyout? Give generously and start another business.

Speak Mandarin? Teach a small group.

Empty nester? Pour into a generation.

Living in your childhood hometown? You know more about it than most. Use that knowledge to make a difference.

Can one of your passions meet a need where you live? I'm certain of it.

Our position is significant to the bigger, wider, more creative story God is writing. When the significance of what God can do through you transcends the title society has given you, you are rightly positioned. Be defined by what's on your passion card— your heart and mind—not what's on your business card. You might be positioned as a volunteer, caregiver, room parent, door holder, pianist, grandparent, or intern. What's on Julia's business card is "grant writer." What's on her passion card is "president of a large-city civic organization." What's on Eugenia's business card is "partner." What's on her passion card is "networking for the sake of the kingdom."

Where do you work? What is your position? What kingdom are you operating out of? What are you doing that points others to

Where do you work?

_____

What is your position?

_____

What kingdom are you operating out of?

_____

What are you doing that points others to Him?

_____

Passion Card

God? Write the answers to these questions on the "passion card" above. For example, mine might say: San Francisco, mother and writer, kingdom of God, and looking for ways to connect and encourage others to stay and invest in this city.

DWELLER TIP

What are you good at? Offer it to your community! I'm a native Spanish speaker, so I teach Spanish once a week to some of our neighborhood kids. We have a lot of fun, and it brings us closer together.

—Lidia, stay-at-home mom

be a dweller of purpose

• • • • • •

I will most gladly spend and be spent for your souls.

2 Corinthians 12:15

21

Connector

Where you live is where you *dwell*. The Middle English origin of the word implies tarrying and lingering. Sticking around for a while. Dwellers live in a particular way. They see the land as deep and wide. Dwellers are never satisfied with "this is just how it is." Dwellers have purpose, want more, and step into making that more a reality. Fredrick Buechner said it this way: "The place God calls you to is the place where your deep gladness and the world's deep hunger meet."[1] Dwellers live sent as connectors, storytellers, grace givers, intercessors, and caretakers.

Standing on the brink of the Pacific Ocean, I see where heaven touches earth. The horizon is a distant, fine line. The colors of sky and sea are almost identical, making it difficult to tell at what point heaven becomes earth and earth becomes heaven. Connections happen when we see heaven and earth collide. When we see God connect the dots.

Connections are evident in how Jesus taught us to pray, "Your kingdom come, your will be done, on earth as it is in heaven" (Matt. 6:10). We're to live expectant that what God is up to in heaven will be unleashed on earth. We are the dwellers to bring this about, through His grand and omnipotent orchestration. He's moving people all around, setting us up, positioning us. Do you see it?

God has been connecting us since the foundation of the earth. Connections start with small beginnings, small settings. If we start to focus on our quadrants, circles, and hubs, we'll start to see connections.

Four Connector Stories

Gayle

My favorite pair of jeans had one hole too many, and it was time for a new pair. So before I had to start from scratch with a different pair, I went to eBay with the brand, size, year, and season information. Lo and behold, someone was selling an identical pair in San Francisco! We met in person and exchanged jeans for cash after our introduction. As we did, we shared quick versions of our stories, and Gayle told me she was looking for a church. I told her where we met, our service times, and the website she could go to for more information. Not long after, Gayle came to our church. Now she stands at our front door to welcome others. She told me that the week she sold those jeans was the very week she told her sisters that she just had to find a church home soon. God was orchestrating it all. Her need for a faith family and my need for jeans led to this connection.

Linda

I call Linda the Great Connector. She wouldn't call herself that, but everyone who is her beneficiary would. When we were deciding where to plant a church, Linda was our San Francisco contact. She connected us to believers in the city on our initial trip and to Andy, the planter of Echo Church in Silicon Valley. Andy connected Ben to Pastor Steve Stroope, pastor of LakePointe

Church, Rockwall, Texas. Both churches partnered with us because of Linda's connection.

Praise was certain that God wanted her to trade coasts and call San Francisco home. Her first contact in the area was Linda, who connected Praise to our family. Soon after, a student from Inner Mongolia moved to the city in need of a roommate. Linda was the connector again. Praise and Claire have been friends ever since, and even hold parties to commemorate their friendship with dozens of others who they have met in their time in the city. It was a joy to find a seat by Linda on a green velvet sofa, watching everyone celebrate. She's still in the art of connecting—of bringing heaven and earth together.

Rekha

Why did the chocolate chip cookie go to the doctor? Because he was feeling crummy. That's all our son, Asher, remembered before he dozed off so the doctor could remove his adenoid. A sweet nurse stayed by his side for the better part of an hour, ready to take care of him when he awoke. I had nothing to do but wait while Asher rested peacefully. So when the nurse looked up, why not engage her in conversation?

"How long have you worked as a nurse?" I asked.

"Just a few weeks. I moved here from the East Coast." From her demeanor, she seemed happy to talk, so I kept going.

"I can remember what that feels like. We moved here several years ago, and it was hard."

The nurse shared about her close-knit family and the relationship that brought her to the city.

"We moved far from family too. But we've made a new family here."

She thought I was talking about our patient!

I laughed and clarified. "He was made in Alabama!"

The nurse smiled and checked on Asher's vital signs.

"We do have four kids," I said, "and that makes for a big family, especially here, but I'm talking about our church family."

The nurse melted. She found comfort in releasing her next words.

"I was a part of a special church community back east." She paused. "I haven't found one here."

It was with great joy that I told her about our family. How we gather on Sundays and meet in small groups during the week. How we take meals to each other and spend holidays together in the city when we can't get back home.

"You should come sometime," I said, when I had finished.

Asher started stirring. We both looked at our patient. His head was facing me.

As he opened his eyes, he spoke slowly, "Mom, this Sunday." He woke some more. "Tell her to come this Sunday—to see me get baptized."

I gazed from Asher to the nurse. She had heard every mumbled word. I had forgotten about the baptism with the surgery at the forefront of my mind. Asher had made his very own decision to follow Jesus, and this upcoming Sunday he was being baptized.

"I'd love to come, Asher," she told him.

He did his best to smile with his very sore throat.

"I'm Rekha," she said.

"I'm Shauna."

Asher's first words to Ben were about the invitation he had just given to Rekha, his recovery nurse.

Guess who came up to the front of the room after Asher's baptism that Sunday? Rekha and her boyfriend.

Not all conversations lead to people coming to church. Not all conversations are supposed to. But all of them can lead us to stepping into their world and them stepping into ours. It's quite miraculous when heaven and earth collide, and Jesus gets all the credit.

Sam's Teacher

It was our son Sam's day to be the star. He could bring his family to his kindergarten class and create an "All about Me" poster. He chose to include a picture of our Compassion International–sponsored child, Saddam. The teacher took notice. Over the holidays, she asked if we could meet for breakfast. Her heart had been stirring for years for the hungry and needy children of the world. But all the commercials and campaigns had left her suspicious. She wanted to know how and why we helped Saddam. I left nothing to the imagination. I shared Compassion's tagline, which is "releasing children from poverty in the name of Jesus." She talked it over with her husband, and they decided to sponsor a girl named Sarah. Summer came, and I let Sam's teacher know that I would be meeting our sponsored child and would love to take anything to Sarah on her behalf. She filled a backpack with a dress, basic supplies, and everything else a schoolteacher knew a child could use. Saddam and Sarah go to school together in Uganda. We got to personally hand the backpack to Sarah and watch her pull out one item at a time. Sarah's mom looked on with such delight. A schoolteacher is changing the life of a young girl halfway around the world because a student of hers displayed a picture of his family that naturally included a young boy in Africa.

Sowing and Reaping

I'd noticed that a blind man about my age walked by our house at the same time every day. I assumed he was on his way to work, and a day came when my routine crossed his routine. We made introductions quickly and walked to the train station together. He was catching a corporate bus to work. I was taking the train downtown. I took a chance and asked if he knew my blind friend Jordyn. (You know her by now!) Guess what? They both worked in the same department! He told me later that he went into the office that day and started singing my name to Jordyn. She was very excited to hear about this connection too.

Connecting is putting into action the sowing principle that Christ taught on earth. This lesson was for the disciples, occurring between Jesus talking with the woman from Samaria and her bringing the townspeople back with her.

In John's Gospel, Jesus said to His disciples, "I sent you to reap that for which you did not labor. Others have labored, and you have entered into their labor" (4:38). Jesus tells the guys that there's plenty to be done and no time to waste. He points out that one day the sower and reaper will rejoice together.

For now, we play our part as connectors. Jesus doesn't have an age requirement or a time frame for how long you have to live somewhere to serve as a connector. He's using four kids in San Francisco at their schools, on their sports fields, and in places they aren't expecting.

I can ask a family on the train if they're going somewhere fun because I have a connection as a mother. But my conversation won't last long if the subject is canines. I've got nothing for you. Think about what gives you a connection among your neighbors, in your quadrants. Speak up in confidence that God will use who you are to draw out the best in others. God sees the sparks flying all over the place as we become the connectors linking heaven and earth, the temporary and the eternal.

We don't always see both sides of the connection, so let's take a look back at the apostle Paul, just moments after his name change, and Ananias, a Damascus city-dweller. In what is commonly seen as his conversion experience, Saul is told by God to "rise and enter the city" (Acts 9:6). He was originally headed that way to stop the spread of Christianity, but encountered God. With Saul's record, I get why God didn't tell him everything in that blinding moment. About the same time, God told Ananias, "Go, for [this man] is a chosen instrument of mine" (v. 15). Here we have a believer being told to find this unbeliever to lead him into truth.

Who is God connecting you to?

Both were told to *go*. From God's perspective (now our perspective), Saul was being led to Christ in the city and Ananias was being led to Saul because of Christ. They would meet and connect because of God's grand orchestration. Living sent is listening and being attuned to the Spirit by going and obeying without knowing the end result.

Who has recently come into your world and needs to see Jesus in you?

Write your name on one line and their name on the other. I have Shauna and Gayle. Linda and Praise. Asher and Rekha. Jesus is our Connector by way of the cross.

DWELLER TIP

Health and fitness matter, and with no gym in our small town, we turned our driveway and garage into a boot camp, inviting over the neighbors and church folk.

—Mike and Mickey, pastor's family in Bryan, Ohio

22

Storyteller

Hold up your pointer finger and trace the skyline you see. It might be as rigid as mine. Perhaps it's rolling hills or level farmland. Its height might cap at two-story buildings, billboard signs, or a water tower. These outlines mark the boundaries of where we live, where our stories take place. Our stories look different from each other's, and that's a good thing. We're filling up a kingdom library, and God desires diversity. No book is the same. Each one is unique. We share our stories to show others what God is doing in our corner of the world. We pass them down to the next generation to make known what God has done in our family. These stories are part of the history of our dwelling place, a record of the faithfulness of God.

Our communities are built on stories of how people endured, persevered, fought, defended, stood up, broke ground, carved roads, instituted this, and established that. Historical markers, statues, ruins, and museums commemorate the people and places that built stories before us. Where are those places in your town?

Your City Has a Story

Dr. Maya Angelou once lived where I live. She was the city's first female and African American cable car conductor—at the age of fourteen. Etched in stone along the Jack Kerouac Alley are Angelou's words: "Without courage we cannot practice any other virtue with consistency."[1] She is a part of our city's history.

Travel southwest, and almost central in the city is the highest hill, Mount Davidson. Atop Mount Davidson is one of the world's tallest crosses. This concrete cross is hidden among the forest. You have to be looking for it to see it. I'm certain not all of my fellow citizens even know about it. It doesn't make the tourist list like the seals and the cable cars. This concrete cross has replaced a wooden cross that was burned down multiple times in the early to mid-1900s. George Decatur, a Western Union Telegraph Company employee who was also the director of the YMCA, was instrumental in the first Easter sunrise service held at the base of this cross, which five thousand people attended in 1923. On March 25, 1934, one week before Easter, President Franklin D. Roosevelt pressed a golden telegraph key in Washington DC to light up the cross in front of a gathering of fifty thousand.[2] When I look up and see the very tip of that cross, I hear those before me quote the words of Paul: "I planted the seed, Apollos watered it, but God has been making it grow" (1 Cor. 3:6 NIV). The city isn't known for its Christian heritage, but it was the citizens before me who fought hard to build that cross and keep it where it stands.

The place you live has history. Tell its stories as a means to connect with its citizens and to the place you live. Listen to those who have lived there longer when they share what they know. My city is what it is today because of the people who have shaped it. So is yours.

Find Your Story in the City

Will and Bea Moraza entered a city-sponsored housing lottery to buy one of seven apartments at below-market rate, four of which had two bedrooms. Almost three hundred entered. The city agency literally drew names out of a shoebox. Will and Bea were number twenty-six in line. They were told not to lose heart, because every applicant had to be approved first by the city and then by a bank for a loan. Months went by. They surrounded themselves with friends who hoped together. They opened up their story to any and all who would listen as a way of demonstrating faith, not certain of the outcome but certain of the One in control. We were drawn in. It was like waiting for the next season of a show on Netflix. How would God act? Was this the place the Morazas were to live? They got a call. The city was asking for some more paperwork. Did this mean that a large number of the applicants before them weren't eligible? We prayed while Will and Bea did their part of providing documents. Previously, they had a home foreclosure in Florida, which wouldn't look good to the banks. They knew that God needed to be present in every conversation and transaction. It was six months after the lottery when they got the call that one of the apartments was theirs to purchase—one with two bedrooms! Glory to God! There is no other way this could have happened!

Come upstairs with me. They are happy for us to take a look. Isn't it gorgeous? They can see the bay and the sparkling bridge at night. The Morazas were sad to leave their neighbors in a different part of the city but rejoice that they are homeowners in such a competitive and expensive market. More than that, their faith was tested and their story heard by hundreds—and no one gets credit for this but God. Their son, Honor, sums it up well: "It was a big miracle, really—it kept taking little miracles and little miracles. And now we're living in the miracle. It's really amazing at how God works."

The story that God is writing for your life is worth sharing, and He wants to be present in the storytelling. What you would call mundane and ordinary, God calls significant and sacred. My small, rural upbringing has helped me connect with people in an urban setting. My role as pastor's wife, which seems scary to me, has been used by God as inviting to others. Research from Princeton shows that when we tell the stories we are living and have lived to others, it has the same effect on the listener's brain as it does on the storyteller's life. This research also says that the simpler the story, the more likely it will stick.[3]

While you're living sent, some people will be attracted to your lifestyle and life choices. These are the ones who are easier to talk to about your faith, because they're curious. These are no-brainers! By all means, share your story. Why you live here. What you enjoy doing in the city. How you're contributing and settling in.

But others will be uncomfortable and unimpressed with your lifestyle and life choices. While you may not be able to have conversations with them about your faith, they are still watching how you live, parent, work, and give.

My story in the city includes Karen at the nail spa, as I learn her family values of Vietnam. It includes Nancy at the library, who has sent her only child off to college on the East Coast. It is supported by my gym friends and school moms and clerks at the grocery store.

Our faith is built on stories of those who have invited us in, loved us, prayed for us, and blessed us. The faith stories of others will be built on what you have done for them out of your love for Christ.

Engagement and interaction with the desire to display the love of Christ leads to such rich stories—*to be continued* stories, *only God* stories. Like all well-written stories, scenes that must set the stage are followed by scenes that wow us. You can tell her story or his story, their story or the breaking news, but what we all want is a personal story only you can share. Paul Zak, the director of the Center for Neuroeconomics Studies at Claremont Graduate University, says, "Stories that keep people's attention have to be character-driven."[4] So I would ask, where is Jesus in your story?

Find Jesus in Your Story

The woman from Samaria would have said she didn't quite have her life together and that her story was better off private, but when she met Jesus, her life had purpose. She didn't sit with Jesus for hours at the well getting the wording just right before she told the folks in her town. She left her jar and said to everyone, "Come and see."

I can say those three words. *Come and see.*

A testimony is telling your story, testing it out. Your faith story matters. This leads to people encountering Jesus firsthand. It was her story—*her* story that led the people to believe in Jesus. You don't have to know everything about Jesus to invite others to know Him. She could have thought of every reason not to talk to the townspeople about what she had just experienced. But the Jesus she had encountered was more valuable than what others thought of her. My pastor husband says that when we share with other people, we don't say their no for them. Give them a chance to say yes.

Tell the story of the city. Share the comeback after being the underdog team. Describe the miracles that followed a tragedy in town. These won't make breaking news on NBC or flow through the ticker line on CNN, but they are breaking praise in the heavens.

God gives us stories to tell. What He is doing and has done in our very lives is what He desires us to use. Yes, even the painful and vulnerable stories. It's the enemy who wants you to view your story as a dud or a waste. When we speak our story, when we verbally empathize with someone because we've been there, we bring power to our story and attention to the One who is writing it.

When I read Jesus's commission for us all to go and make disciples in Matthew 28:19–20, I hear Him say, "Go tell your stories." Because what God has done for me is worth telling to someone else, and what God has done in someone else is worth hearing. For a storyteller is a story listener.

DWELLER TIP

Our girls are fluent in English and Mandarin Chinese, giving them the privilege of communicating with over one billion people on earth. I remind them, "Think about how many people you get to share your story with!"

—Joyce Wong, mom in Singapore

23

Grace Giver

When I don't love where I live, my compassion is the first thing to go. Everyone seems out to get me. They're either in my way or aren't doing what I need them to do. I'm back to the *me* and *them* mentality. I fail to see them as neighbors and instead see them as a nuisance. I fear them, avoid them, and have no desire to understand them. These might be strong words, but it's what happens when this place isn't doing it for me anymore and I feel like the people have failed me.

When we get to this point, we all need a gentle grace reminder. What Jesus lavished on us is ours to lavish on our cities and towns. To live sent is to give grace. To recognize that all we have and all we are comes from God and is not ours for the hoarding but rather for the dispersing.

If we take the posture of Christ, we love because He first loved us. We don't wait for our city to apologize for not throwing us a party when we moved in or to congratulate us for serving at the homeless shelter or to pat us on the back for checking in on our elderly neighbor.

How did Jesus, prior to the cross, give grace and mercy to people? He expected nothing in return; He knew there was nothing the people could give Him that compared to the greatness of the Father; He got all He needed from God. We need grace to give grace.

What does it look like to love a people and a place that have failed you? How do we give them a second or third or fourteenth chance? Is it possible for us to do for others what Jesus Himself did for us? Is it possible to do as Proverbs 3:27 says: "Do not withhold good . . . when it is in your power to do it"?

Give and Take with Grace

Joseph gave grace away when we'd understand if he responded differently. He gave grace in the very land where he had doubted God's presence and experienced pain from his family, his employer, and guys he thought were his friends. He chose to bless the land where he had spent so much time isolated and misunderstood.

He told his brothers to come close, for he had a story to tell them—a story of the certainty that God had sent him to the palace despite his brothers' evil intentions. The days that led to this moment had been hard and only got worse before they got better. He was in a physical place he didn't choose to be, but God did. And when he tried to get out by way of the cupbearer, the baker, and service to Potiphar, he couldn't. God was doing something, and Joseph had to stay put and stay faithful. But he was ready when he was called upon. Joseph would be given so much responsibility that would affect his family, a people, and a land. He could vividly recall years of solitude, questioning, doubting, and longing for his previous home—to be at the table with his dad, to have brothers that loved him, to return to the fields. But he said, "God sent me ahead of you to preserve for you a remnant on earth and to save your lives by a great deliverance" (Gen. 45:7 NIV).

My first reaction to the gracelessness of others is to want to run away to those greener pastures.

Our friends Cory and Brett both ran to the city for work and to escape what they had known, but they found more of God here than any other time in their lives. It's not that they were running from God; they just couldn't fathom that more of God was theirs for the taking. That's grace.

My friend Chelsey lives more in the upfront-in-your-face brokenness in our city. She preaches that when the city doesn't deliver, she's looking at the wrong deliverer. When she plays the scenario out in her mind of moving elsewhere, to a more quaint location, she knows that, given time, it won't deliver for her either.

Psalmist David recognized God as the true Deliverer when he prayed, "As for me, I am poor and needy, but the Lord takes thought for me. You are my help and my deliverer; do not delay, O my God!" (Ps. 40:17). Our grace place, our deliverance, is found in Him. And He is found by calling on His name.

Our Access to Grace

The Hebrew word for grace is *chen*, and the Greek word is *charis*. It literally means *favor, to bend or stoop in kindness to another as a superior to an inferior*.[1] Jesus is the superior one who stooped down for us, making Himself inferior, giving grace and mercy.

How do we come close to give grace? God and Moses chatted about this. Let's listen in.

God said, "[I am] merciful and gracious, slow to anger, and abounding in steadfast love and faithfulness." He then pointed out sin among the people that can't coexist in His presence.

Moses bent low. He worshiped God and sought His favor (grace) and His forgiveness (mercy) on behalf of the people.

God responded, "Behold, I am making a covenant. Before all your people I will do marvels, *such as have not been created in all the earth or in any nation.* And all the people among whom you are shall see the work of the Lord, for it is an awesome thing that I will do *with* you" (Exod. 34:6, 8–10, emphasis added).

How good is God? He tells us who He is and what He can't be around. Moses agreed with what God said, and on behalf of the people who lived among him, he asked for grace and mercy. And what did God do? Do you see it because you too have experienced it? God, in the richness of grace, said He was going to do something He'd never done before, that no man had done before. And He was going to do so *with* Moses. No other religion exists where the Creator stands with His created to draw others to Himself. He calls us to give grace right alongside Him! Love others out of this truth, for when we forget this profound identity, we cease to live sent with purpose.

We follow God through the day not to earn His grace but out of the love we have for Him because of His grace. Will we mirror that to our city? Will we love and give grace out of a relationship with the Grace Giver?

Our Interruptions Are Grace-Giving Moments

Our family has a pretty normal weekday routine that takes us up and down the same streets to get to school and work. One particular day, we were sitting at a traffic light facing north when *pow*! I had caught a glimpse out of my peripheral vision and I knew something had come at me. In a matter of seconds, I made sure the kids were okay and then went to open my door. It wouldn't budge. I looked out of my window to see a man attempting to get up and then walk. He made it over to the sidewalk, carrying his skateboard. I climbed over seats to get out of the passenger door. My heart raced. He was okay. His ribs ached, but his pride was the most scuffed up, he told me. He had skateboarded down the hill to get to the bus stop, like usual. Today should have been no different. Except he didn't make the turn and had crashed into our van sitting at the traffic light.

We exchanged contact information, as the van would need some repair and he would need some prayer. A week went by, and our van was back to normal. I know his week wasn't as smooth as ours, though. I reached out and asked if we could bring him and his wife a meal. I had learned that they had recently moved to the city from the Midwest, and I knew that feeling all too well. We met at his home, just up the hill from the crash. He reported that he was on the mend and was grateful for a hot meal. I wanted him to know more than anything that we were finding community in this fast-paced environment. I told him of our church family and that we would continue to pray for his full recovery. Now when we drive up and down the hills, we see skateboard Greg—minus the skateboard. Yes, we're the people who roll down our windows and say, "Hi, Greg!" and he waves back.

Dwellers of purpose, we are His image-bearers and therefore we are grace givers. Our natural inclination is for others to serve us. But when we're living on purpose, God is setting us up to serve others.

Nothing is routine and all of it is by God's grace. Henri Nouwen described it this way: "My whole life I have been complaining that my work was constantly interrupted, until I discovered my interruptions were my work."[2]

The Tale of One Anothers

People have flocked to my city for years because they are misfits elsewhere. Earlier people sailed to America because they wanted out of bondage and to worship as they pleased. Neighboring countries open their doors to refugees. We all long to call a place home among people who don't judge us but accept us. Who extend mercy rather than condemnation. There is no condemnation in Christ Jesus. Whew! Then there is none for me to give, either.

Jesus said, "A new commandment I give to you, that you love one another: just as I have loved you, you also are to love one another" (John 13:34). Grace doesn't come with names but is labeled for the *one anothers* we encounter. Who are the *one anothers* in your community? I'll go first.

One of my son's classmates, who just wouldn't stop picking on him.

The man who takes my parking spot, leaves me dumbfounded, and then proceeds to tell me with pity, "We're not going to talk about this, are we?" He walks away.

The people I don't understand.

Someone who speaks unkindly to my husband.

It's a relief that judging is not up to me. I'm free of the gavel and the courtroom. I'm free to head to the streets, office, and living room and put others first, give them grace. Because God has called me to be a mercy giver. He is the judge. I get to give mercy and show mercy. I'm not bound to my past and don't possess the chains to hold others there either. We have the keys to freedom, to love, to releasing His compassion—an unlimited resource.

This adventure is not a bed of roses but a choice to thrive among the thorns. Strike up a conversation across the aisle, across the street. What if life has been really lonely for that neighbor? Say hello. He was beginning to wonder if anyone even noticed him. This doesn't keep you from your job; it keeps you in the rhythm of your purpose—that all may know Him. For when the gap between who we are and what He's calling us to do is great, so are the opportunities for grace to abound.

DWELLER TIP

Which one would you strike up a conversation with in a long line—the lady ahead of you with the cross necklace or the man behind you with the tattoo and body piercing? Be a blessing to both.

—RM

24

Intercessor

Scoop up the earth. Let the minuscule pieces fall through your fingers. Rise up. Look around you. This land has been given to you. You are the intercessors in the land—the ones who intervene. Intercession is:

The very link between God's heart and humanity.

A voice on behalf of the people.

Coming under the mighty hand of God with hands out toward those we bring before Him.

A powerful expression of involvement in the lives of others.

Engagement without always making an introduction.

We often neglect prayer (our part) to try to control the day (God's part). Doing our part connects to the whole—the whole story God has been writing, the song He's been orchestrating since before time began. As intercessors, we speak from having been with the Father. Start now in the season of life you're in. For we are storybooks contained in flesh personified. The stories that fill this book are birthed from intercession. The people of our cities will know us by our love, and that love starts with talking to God about them.

Pray in the Land in Which You Live

If you're having a hard time learning to love where you live, intercede. Set your needs aside to elevate the needs of others by taking the posture of an intercessor—a bowed heart, with eyes open and a fervent prayer on your lips. This prayer warms our hearts to the people of our cities. We can grow a love for our towns that will develop through prayer.

Intercession has everything to do with the land on which you stand. We feel the weight of the burdens of our cities more strongly than those who don't live here. We pray differently over our culture because we live among it. This is part of God's reason for you being here. We can see the city change for the better through the prayers of His people. I can tell someone that I'm praying for them as they live in Hilo, Hawaii, but their prayers can grab the heart of God over an issue in their community differently than mine can. I can ask someone to pray for the city of San Francisco, but because I'm walking it and feeling it, touching it and being affected by it, I can pray more raw and honestly.

Evil is in this world. We hear of it and experience it, and our hearts sink in despair. Dwellers of purpose, we are not the hopeless but the hope-filled. We face the evil with intercessory prayer. Evil can't be extinguished with anger or frustration or enough conversations with friends or through social media. We don't stop battling. God will overcome all evil one day once and for all, but in our time here on earth, we push back the darkness by calling on the God of this universe to enter our homes, our businesses, our schools, our towns. Through the longevity and consistency of dwelling, our influence and intercession can cover global ground.

Think Like a Soldier

Rees Howells now resides in the heavenly city, but he once dwelled in South Africa and Wales, where he lived as a miner, missionary, and later founder of the Bible College of Wales. Intercession is how Howells lived every day, sometimes every hour. During World War II, he would intercede for the soldiers. Rees chose to do so by living and thinking like them. The troops had no holidays, days off, or time with family; ate rations; and were on guard through the night. For a season, Rees also took no rest but battled for peace and protection. He also prayed strategically against evil. "Prevail against Hitler," he prayed for three weeks, with fasting.[1] "War seemed inescapable, and the leaders of the nation called for a day of prayer." Howells saw it as a test of strength between the devil in Hitler and the Holy Spirit in His army of intercessors. "Lord, bend Hitler," was his cry, among others.[2] When it was written in the *South Wales Evening Post* that God had averted a European War when the Munich Agreement was signed, people wondered what had happened to Hitler. Sir Nevile Henderson, the British ambassador to Germany, wrote, "Hitler felt irritated with himself. . . . There, for the first time, he had been compelled to listen to contrary opinion."[3] Howells knew the Lord had bent Hitler. Time and time again, Howells interceded by claiming battles belonged to God rather than the enemy. He prayed that the men at Dunkirk would be safe, and leaders would say that God had intervened at Dunkirk.[4]

Rees Howells joins a long list of contemplatives, beginning with the desert fathers, who saw their chosen life not as a removal from the world but instead as a way of engaging with God on behalf of the world, for the world.[5] That long list includes the people who gathered at Wednesday night prayer meeting at my childhood church. As the smell of buttered rolls and fried chicken filled the fellowship hall, so did their prayers. I saw them as older people sharing their woes, but rather they were intercessors wanting updates to share the load and see God work and heal. I wondered how they knew everything about everyone in town. It's because they prayed so much.

How do you know if you are interceding? You feel it. Deeply. Intercession brings about a weightiness. It's a compassionate prayer of stepping into someone else's world and taking on empathy. It's what we do with this weight and burden that makes intercession complete. We feel the needs of a person, take them to God in prayer, and leave them with Him. As we engage with others, we continue the cycle. Feel the need, take it to God, leave it with Him. Feel the need, take it to God, leave it with Him. He is the One who can take it from us. We will stop interceding when we find ourselves carrying weights that mount and not handing them over to the God who hears. It will be too much to handle. Yet there's a perk to intercession that we often fail to see, the result of wearing down the path between God and those we are interceding for.

The Gift of Intercession Is Seeing God

San Francisco students attend the school of their choice, not a school assigned according to where they live. Theoretically. Think seventy-plus elementary schools and a city that values free choice. A student has the option of listing their top schools and, through a lottery, the computer generates that student's placement. Having moved in the summer, we missed this application process. When it was my turn in line at the school district office, it was clear to me that God led the conversation with the counselor. I know because I'd heard nightmares of this process. I was suited up for battle. For months we had prayed and felt the burden for a people we'd yet to meet and a process we didn't fully understand. I was prepared for anything but was surprised by what God was doing before my very eyes. When the counselor began to tell me my options, I stopped her at the first name. It was one of the public schools we had been praying for.

"We'll take it," I blurted out. I'm certain my excitement frightened her.

With the assignment in hand, I darted back to the van where Ben was waiting. We couldn't believe it. We were living in our answered prayer, but only part of it. More was still to come.

"How is there even a spot at this school?" Ben asked.

"I don't know. She said there was one spot and I took it!"

After Elijah had gone to this school for two years, we stepped deeper into the gift of intercession. He was now a third grader. The boys were playing on the playground one afternoon while I chatted with one of our teachers. She paused our conversation to welcome a former student, who had recently returned from Europe.

"This family had to leave after only being at school for four days," she told me. She went on to say that the father's job had moved them back to Europe for two years, but they had now returned, and it was a miracle that the little girl was able to return to the same school. (Everyone in San Francisco is aware of the school lottery craziness.)

"Mom, that's Dora." Elijah was panting from playground activity. "She's in my class."

She was the one who had created the opening for Elijah to enter the school in first grade. I ran ahead to introduce myself to Dora and her mom.

The gift of intercession was all around, and I was coming undone! This European mom could tell. I got it. Elijah got it. The mom thought it was simply lovely that things worked out for all of us.

We're not promised a visual of the interior workings of prayer. However, I can testify what this did to my faith that day—God was closer than I could imagine. He was uniquely involved in our lives. He cared where our children went to school. He cared about this European family. He moved things around in His timing and in His mysterious ways, and we got to witness it because we interceded.

* * * * * *

Our son Sam was two when we moved, and his friends were all a bit older than him—college students at the University of Alabama. One of his favorites was Josh. In our short time in the Midwest, Josh was a part of Sam's nightly prayers. It was a simple, consistent, two-year intercessory prayer: "God, I pray for Josh." When the word got out that we were moving to the West Coast to start a church, Ben reached out to Josh, as he was finishing up grad school, and Josh decided he would look for a job where we were moving. Josh has always been open to what God was doing around him, be it on a college campus or around the world. He got a job and moved to San Francisco two months before we did. We were mind-blown. Sam wasn't. Intercessory prayer is drenched in hope because dwellers pray believing God for the impossible.

. . . . . .

Our daughter, Kavita, came to us from India as an answer to intercessory prayer. Every place we've ever lived and every person we've ever known called on God to bring this precious girl home. I can think of several friends who prayed to God for the very first time during this journey. The way people responded to this answered prayer is because they had positioned themselves between God and us for three years. They kept praying through the silence of a year of no referral. They rejoiced on the day we knew her name and saw her picture as if they too had gained a daughter. They felt the pain that came when she was denied to our family. They grew frustrated when the courts took a recess and when months went by before a new judge was assigned to our case. As Ben and I traveled to India, their intercessory prayers were equally as valuable as our passports. They were needed to get Ben into the country, because of his occupation. These prayers sustained me when I was sick and when Kavita clung to the hotel window with massive confusion about what was happening to her.

Saddam even prayed for Kavita to come home to her forever family. For three years, he would write and tell us he was praying for her. He had a family. Not a complete one, like I wanted for him. He had his basic needs met, but I wanted more for him. Yet he wasn't fixated on his needs. He was interceding for hers. He had a family, and he wanted Kavita to have one too. Our sponsored child in Kampala, Uganda, prayed for an orphaned girl in India. Saddam rejoiced when he received the picture of our family of six. He'd helped pray her home. He saw the gift of intercession. One day I'm certain Saddam will meet Kavita.

One O'clock in the Afternoon

After Jesus left the Samaritan well, He went back to the town of Cana, where he had performed his first miracle, turning water into wine. Just as place matters, so does time. A father who was also a government official came to Jesus asking for healing over his son. Jesus said, "Your son will live." The dad believed at one o'clock in the afternoon. It was another day before he arrived back at home, where he had last seen his very sick son—who no longer was very sick.

He spoke with his servant and asked when he had made a turn for the better.

"One o'clock," the servant told him (John 4:46–53).

God's orchestration! His grand orchestration! The miracle of intercession is when prayer is lifted to God and He releases His power on earth.

Seven-ish in the Morning

We're not the only ones who have a weekday morning routine with a give-and-go on the brakes through dozens of stop signs and traffic lights. We often see the same faces, and have names for them. There's "the librarian." She parks her car near the park and walks downhill to the train station. She's probably a makeup artist, but she very much resembles a librarian. "That guy" is a morning person. He's got his headphones on and is grinning big.

We try to guess what song he is listening to. He's typically wearing all black with a splash of red. Even his clothing is routine. We pray for "the librarian," "that guy," and "skateboard Greg" on our morning weekday drives. Because they live where we live. They have a story. They matter to us, and they matter to God. I believe God intersects our routine with their routines so we can talk to Him about them. We might be the only ones praying for them. I pray they are headed into environments where Christians are loving and serving them.

Strategic Prayers

Tricia Neill says, "God will use the Scriptures and prayer to spark our hearts and imaginations with the first flames of a vision and, as we pray, and as we listen, the vision that God has for us begins to take shape."[6] Here are ways to intercede:

- Pray the Scriptures. It's already written. Substitute names and places. I choose to pray Psalm 130:7–8 over my city: "O San Francisco, hope in the LORD! For with the LORD there is steadfast love, and with him is plentiful redemption. And he will redeem San Francisco from all its iniquities."

- Say His Name. *Jesus.* Try it. Say it out loud. I realize someone will probably hear you. This one name, this one word can release all the power in heaven. Prayer is not restricted to the table or always accompanied by Bible reading. It goes with you throughout the day.

- Pray in response to God and what you think He's doing. Our prayer list is ongoing and can feel insurmountable. Too much to cover in a matter of twenty-four hours. Rather, as you say good morning to your spouse, ask God to lead them today. As you wake the kids, pray that they would notice Him near them and fighting for them today. When a name comes to your mind, give it to God.

- Open your front door. Welcome Jesus in, for prayer leads to love. Ask God to bring believers to your neighborhood. Stand at the entrance of your office. Smile at those who pass you by. Go ahead and do a 360 from your desk, giving every person in view up to God. Positions open in your company? Ask God to bring men and women of integrity there. Utter this prayer: "Jesus, You are welcome here." Invite Him in through prayer. It's how He responds to our requests and how we recognize ways to engage with people.

- Intercessory prayer invites God into the situation. If you're praying for someone, why not pray with that someone? "Can I pray with you?" They'll likely say yes and might even reach out to God in prayer later. You made God approachable.

Know He is praying for you. Intercession was Jesus's strategy while He lived here: "I am praying for them. I am not praying for the world but for those whom you have given me, for they are yours" (John 17:9). He still does so through the Holy Spirit. Let's find comfort when we don't know what to pray, because "the Spirit intercedes for the saints according to the will of God" (Rom. 8:27).

DWELLER TIP

A prayer before my workout at the gym, a mention of going to church to my aesthetician, questioning secular viewpoints in class, posting a biblical message on social media. I now welcome Jesus into places where I didn't think to before, and He's showing up!

—Michelle, PhD student

25

Caretaker

We had to get out of town. And soon. I was up to my elbows in concrete and needed to be surrounded by all things green. With every mile out of the city, my shoulders dropped a degree. I was sinking into rest. I just didn't know how bad it was until I opened the passenger door of the van and stepped out onto the dirt path that led to a cabin hours from home. Oh goodness—tears began to fall. I had lost all control. I was able to take deep breaths of pine. Fresh air rushed down my throat. My soul was receiving nourishment. I was so completely on empty that just taking a few breaths probably could have returned me to the city better than I left it. But we were just getting to the cabin in the woods with friends from the city, and I wasn't the only one with a tear issue.

Our friend translated what I was experiencing. "The city has worn on us. This is how we know we are entering rest." For the next few days, we had no indoor plumbing nor electricity. The sun would set and lanterns would be required for board games and late night snacks. As we all settled into sleep, I don't ever recall the dark being so dark. Our souls were light though. Nightlife lulled us to sleep as the critters made conversation without us. We received the rest. For when we rest, we receive.

I've come to quote Mark Batterson's simple formula on every exodus from the city: "A change of pace plus a change of place equals a change of perspective."[1] He says that where we are geographically affects where we are spiritually. I consider it a prerequisite insight.

I remember another time of seeking rest in the mountains. On this particular escape I didn't get the perspective I was subconsciously hoping for. I was hoping that the hours away would be the salve my soul needed, but what I was longing for was back in the city. The very fresh mountain air that I was inhaling as rest was the same air that was suffocating our oldest son. He was having a hard time breathing the thin air. We needed to cut our trip short so we could get him to our pediatrician. We had a few good days away, but as we crossed the bridge back into the city, I cried. Coming back was relief for our son, for he would get medical liquid for his lungs, and that made me smile through the tears. But it was too soon for me. I wasn't ready to come back to the place we'd been sent to love. I had to learn to find rest in the city when escaping to the mountains wasn't a possibility. Living sent was sucking the life out of me, and I needed to learn to rest where I lived.

Rest Where You Live

I'm all for escaping before you explode and driving miles out of town to gain clarity, get away, change it up, and relax. But that might not be your reality until three months from now. What equals rest to you in your city limits?

We have different rest languages, but we have the same Rest Giver. Withdraw. Be still. A space that is different from routine can speak rest. Our calendars fill up, and we crowd out rest. It's the first thing we think we can do without, so it gets bumped, and we tell ourselves we'll make up for it later. Rest is intentionally going to places where you live that help you inhale and exhale deeper. It's a pick-me-up. Coffee with a friend. Sunshine. Maybe you've been out all week, and home equals rest. Enter it as such. It can happen with your Bible or Bible app and five or ten minutes. I grew up calling this a quiet time, but it's never completely quiet for me. If you're like me, you're outnumbered by kids in your home. Taking rest can happen in the bedroom closet by closing the door, taking on Christ's mind and His promises that He counts as an authority in your home, and getting back out there. You're not outnumbered when He's on your side.

No matter how densely or lightly populated our physical locations may be, we need clear minds, uncluttered souls, and responsive hearts to be awakened to God's purpose for our lives. We find this when we come to Him for rest. There will be seasons and circumstances when a longer stint of rest, a sabbatical, or counseling are needed. Caretaking is for the day-to-day so you can stay in your race.

In finding rest we take C.A.R.E. of ourselves: Come to Jesus. Acknowledge the tension. Repent and re-center. Enter back into the story.

Come to Jesus

I want to take you to my favorite shop down this little alley. It's not that it's hidden. It's just that everything else has crowded in around it. You can tell by the architecture that it's been here awhile, yet the infrastructure is pristine. I don't have to suggest that we go in; you know it looks inviting. Yet the countless other shops can drown this one out. Flashy lights, sale signs—*hurry in and buy today, no down payment*. The line is out the door of the electronics store, and people are swinging their bags from the other retail shops around the corner. We'd have missed this particular shop if we had our devices in hand, trying to keep up with what everyone else is doing and where they're going on vacation.

I push the door open and the bell signals to the shop owner that He has visitors. He is happy to set His work down for anyone who walks in. He's glad we stopped by—it's evident on His face. This place is everything you and I need it to be. It's an escape, a refuge, a contrast to the outside world, inviting, uncondescending, and a sigh of relief. We take a rest—as long as we need to. This shop never closes, and the owner is always here. We've come to the One who made us, who knows us, who called us to salvation, who knows the days we have here on earth, who has our names written on the palm of His hand, who sees us, who sings over us, who comes to our rescue, who delights in us, who died for us and rose again, and who is preparing a home for us in the heavenly city. He sees you and me trying to live with purpose in the very place He has sent us and that brings Him great joy.

You have to be meeting with Jesus to live this lifestyle. How else will you know your purpose? How else will you have the strength? How else will you have the words? How can you see? Mark Buchanan writes:

> If God works all things together for good for those who love him and are called to his purposes, you can relax. If he doesn't, start worrying. If God can take any mess, any mishap, any wastage, any wreckage, any anything, and choreograph beauty and meaning from it, then you can take a day off. If he can't, get busy. Either God's always at work, watching the city, building the house, or you need to try harder. Either God is good and in control, or it all depends on you.[2]

Scripture ties the rest of God to the Word of God, and it ties our rest to His rest.

> So then, there remains a Sabbath rest for the people of God, for whoever has entered God's rest has also rested from his works as God did from his. Let us therefore strive to enter that rest, so that no one may fall by the same sort of disobedience. For the word of

God is living and active . . . discerning the thoughts and intentions
of the heart. (Heb. 4:9–12)

I can sleep easily, by which I mean the minute my head hits
the pillow, I'm out. This is sleep, but *rest* is a deeper issue. What
we fear keeps us from rest or leads us to rest. A biblical proverb
reads, "The fear of the LORD leads to life, and whoever has it rests
satisfied" (Prov. 19:23). To paraphrase St. Augustine, "Our hearts
are restless until they find You."[3] The Son of God said, "Come
to me . . . and I will give you rest" (Matt. 11:28). Rest is finding
satisfaction that we don't have to work for or earn. Rest is hearing
the truest voice. Rest is returning to our Maker.

Acknowledge the Tension

There are times when our errands take us to some rough parts
of our city, and we walk closer to each other with our eyes wide
open. Downtown and in the open, depravity leans against closed
storefronts. People are "smoking smelly stuff," and their minds
are not as sharp as they once were.

These moments bring tension. "I can't fix it all" is that tension's name.

"What do I do with what I see?" was the name of one of our
children's tension. We don't venture out looking for this tension,
but God makes us aware of it as we see the contrasts of light and
dark in our city. Think about what depravity looks like in your
corner of the world.

The tension is the noticeable division of a perfect heaven with
an imperfect earth. A loving father and a wayward child. War and
peace. Brokenness and beauty. Light and dark. With living sent
comes the gift of seeing present day life coupled with a yearning
for eternal life. Our soul aches for people to experience God's
love. We long for peace on earth. We cry out for His mercy. We
intervene for our colleagues, neighbors, families, and friends. As

long as we have our eyes fixed on Jesus, and our lives are being spent for others, we will be found in the tension. That's a telltale sign you're living sent. Trust is our response to a God who sees the tension, holds us tight, yet releases us to be His hands and feet until He comes back. This book has no value if you feel no tension. Living sent is living in the tension, living with the trust.

We struggle with comparison and competition. To have that size ministry, that size budget, that kind of living, that kind of family. Our propensity is to be so distracted by the glitz and glamour of society's offerings that we see stuff and success rather than His plan for redemption and rest. The back and forth from city to suburbs comes from our very own dissatisfaction with what our little gods cannot deliver. The city gets hard, messy, and overcrowded, so we move to the suburbs. The suburbs grow small, opportunities are limited, and diversity shrinks, so we run to the cities. What we need is rest, not a rebound. Living sent requires more of us than we can humanly give. We are emptied out more quickly and have to return to the Spring of Living Water more often. Dwellers are constantly being poured out. So when we have nothing left, we take a rest. It's a dance of resting from work and working from rest.

Acknowledging the struggle disturbs the enemy. It's been his tactic all along to make you feel like you are the only one who struggles, to shut you up, to keep you down, to make you afraid. But when you tell God your struggles, you invite His Spirit of truth to penetrate those dark and dismal places with His light and His strength and His grace. We cannot keep God from knowing our struggles, but we can keep our hearts from resting in Him. He doesn't get tired of hearing from us.

Repent, Re-center

We're afraid to be caught empty-handed. We look more important when we have our hands full. Rest is setting something down and not picking something else up so that we're ready to receive what God wants to give us. Empty hands open us up to identify what is causing the struggle and what rest requires.

Our sin and fleshly struggles need repentance. Repentance is declaring "I've waged war against people, against God and His ways." Our war is not against a people but the principalities of darkness. Repentance is confessing that *me* and *them* mindset. It is asking Jesus to cleanse our thoughts, wash our hands, and change our direction so we go the other way. Repentance is purifying our hearts to better care for ourselves and others.

Our internal struggles can set our mind askew, and we need a re-centering. Re-centering is getting outside of ourselves by allowing God to enter more of us. John Ortberg writes, "A soul centered in God always knows it has a heavenly Father who will hold its pain, its fear, its anxiety. This is spiritual life: to place the soul each moment in the presence and care of God."[4] Yes, life situations might cause disappointment, but they don't have power over our souls. When you think about it this way, you realize that external circumstances cannot keep you from being with God. If anything, they draw you closer to Him.

If you breezed through this chapter, could it be you aren't being emptied to have the need of being filled? The tension feels like weakness, like homesickness, like a heavy burden. Say it is so, and instead of dousing it with social media or nullifying it with gluttony or an impulse buy or packing a suitcase and running, choose a refreshing place in town to get away to and talk to God. Tell Him of your struggles. Tell Him of your pain. Ask Him what you should do.

Enter Back into the Story

Mark tells us that Jesus went to talk to God alone. Then the disciples came looking for Him and said, "Everyone else is looking for you!" Jesus wows me here. He said, "Let's go. This is why I'm here" (Mark 1:37–38). Jesus entered back into the story from a place of rest. We must do the same. Because your story isn't over.

DWELLER TIP

If Christ is our priority, that gives us a compass for decisions we need to make in the midst of busyness. In this, He provides the rest we need.

—The McCords

to be continued

• • • • • •

Your kingdom come, your will be done, on earth as it is in heaven.

Matthew 6:10

26

Your Story Isn't Over

We are the faithful who have a God worth sharing. Christianity is not wrapped up in secrecy but is intended to be lived out in the world God created. Yes, this world is currently broken but it is also one He sent His Son to redeem. Let's be who He's created us to be and dwell where He's called us to stay. For the potential in you is great. With breath in your lungs, your fruit-bearing years are still strong. From intercession to acts of kindness, through your awareness and obedience, you will bear fruit that lasts.

I heard Jill Briscoe, Bible teacher and United Kingdom native, share her story of coming to faith as a young woman through a nurse who was sick in bed beside her at the hospital. As they were lying flat on their backs, the nurse friend said her mission field was the ground under her feet. Immediately Jill started to share her new faith in the hospital, even the little she knew. She said that after obedience, courage was waiting for her. Briscoe gave the challenge to believers to "Go where you're sent, stay where you're put, [and] give what you've got until you're done."[1]

We must recognize He chooses to use us to make Him known in our community. Look for Him and you will find Him. He's been telling His followers this for a long time. We're not superheroes swooping in to save the people. We don't walk in alone or as pioneers into uncharted waters. Jesus has gone before us.

Our time here on earth is to be about God's mission. As we live and move through our days, we have the privilege of catching glimpses of heaven and of our global God. Our stories are developing. We are in the process of leaving our place better than we found it as we pray, tell our stories, give grace, and do life together.

Jesus reminds us:

> The knowledge of the secrets of the kingdom of heaven has been given to you. . . . Blessed are your eyes because they see, and your ears because they hear. For truly I tell you, many prophets and righteous people longed to see what you see but did not see it, and to hear what you hear but did not hear it. (Matt. 13:11, 16–17 NIV)

That's what He wants us to take with us. Good news that is portable, transferable, and speaks all languages. Step into the truest identity He has given you, awaken to your gifts, and tell your story.

Your Story Is His Story

Jesus's life is so rich Scripture can't even hold all the stories: "Now there are also many other things that Jesus did. Were every one of them to be written, I suppose that the world itself could not contain the books that would be written" (John 21:25). Everything Jesus was a part of, every miracle, healing, misfit social engagement, fireside chat—it couldn't all be recorded. Our lives can be just as rich with stories. Stories that matter because we give our time to what matters.

We're entertained by other stories when we think we don't have one ourselves. We binge-read the blog of the family who sold everything to be missionaries. We follow the friend of a friend who is using his artistic talent to glorify God and the one who is creating an environmental product that will help the world. We subscribe to get their adoption updates and newsletters about nonprofit work overseas.

We watch from the sidelines, even cheering them on. "Yeah, you've got this! Prayin' for you!" But to stop there is to fail to see that we've been invited into the same story, the greatest story of all. Awaken. Your story isn't over. You've got a part to play, and it's not on the sidelines. Tell your story of what God has done today. What He's done in the past. What you are trusting Him with for the future.

Find the sweetness in your story. We're prone to hurry ours along by rushing the process. I'm learning that in the midst of the process, in the midst of the gradual, therein lies the determination, the decision, the stretching, and the changing. Process is what makes a story great or tragic. A book is not as enjoyable if you read only the first chapter and the last. It's all the in-between that gives it clarity and character.

My conclusion is this: Jesus came to give us a life here on earth that is full in the most abundant way possible. Since life is a process, it's a continuation of what God is doing and wants to do in you and in everyone around you. This means your story isn't over. And it's right in the middle of the story, in the tension of the process, where we look back at His faithfulness and look forward with His hope.

So Travel with Hope through This Life

As we walk this earth, we travel with hope. Hope is never heavy. In fact, it makes anything else we are carrying feel lightweight. We also travel with Jesus's prayers. While on earth, He prayed for believers to be unified and for our love to be so compelling that it draws others to Him.

Jesus also prays for everyone who will trust in Him because we spoke up, didn't give up, stayed in the process, decided to stay, were intentional in our lifestyle, and dwelled with purpose. The Father's arms are open wide. While He tarries, we point people to Jesus. And when a neighbor moves away or a hairdresser finds a new job, your story isn't over. Keep coming to Jesus for assignments. Stay aware of who He's bringing your way next.

Stay aware of His presence in your life. For God is your Keeper, your Help who "will keep your going out and your coming in from this time forth and forevermore" (Ps. 121:8). This includes the place where He has you (home, present), the place where He takes you (active, down the road), and the place you'll go one day (eternal). May God give us experiences that require us to need His presence more than anything else. Therein lies the hope.

Living sent is bigger than ourselves. What we bring with us is already in us. It is not packaged with fear. What we have in us has been proven faithful, tried and true, for centuries. We carry with us the Spirit of the Living God. Early explorers trusted in it as they sailed uncharted waters. William Wilberforce clung to it as he stood before a government on behalf of an enslaved people. Professional athletes have taken it with them inside locker rooms and into interviews. Students have stepped foot onto school campuses, and along with their backpacks they have this Spirit-given confidence, hope, and favor. Marketing reps, developers, designers, clerks, sitters, health care professionals, bankers, accountants, nonprofit workers, teachers, small business owners, contractors—yes, all of us—greater is He who is in us than he who is in the world.

What is your story? Not the novel-length version but a few clear and concise points that you can have on hand when in conversation. Jot it down right here.

This is my story.

DWELLER TIP

Never let a problem seem too big to solve. While there are many kids living in poverty, help one. I learned one of my students was living in substandard conditions in a trailer with a legally blind grandmother. I made some phone calls to others, who made more phone calls, and this family now has a brand-new home on their property. Their story isn't over. Hopefully, one day this family will understand why we intervened on their behalf.

—April Bagwell, middle school counselor

27

Their Story Isn't Over Either

What if she is just not interested in faith? *What if* he has been hurt by the church? *What if* they only see our differences? *What if* that was my moment and I was too scared to speak? *What if* he falls back into depression when he moves? *What if* it takes her a while to find a church and she falls away from community? *What if* the new is too hard?

Case of the What-Ifs

When life's "what-ifs" threaten to paralyze you, remember the goodness of God and how orchestration is His specialty. He is the sending God of not only you and me but all of us. Our connection, one to another, is how God is growing His kingdom here on earth. Scripture is alive and active, which fuels our faith to be the same. God is moving people all over the globe—shifting plans, leading this person to that person, causing paths to cross. Every person you meet is also a story in progress.

Step foot in a popular gathering spot in your town. Choose to go during a high foot-traffic time of the day. With everyone moving about, toss the *what-ifs* in the air and let God take them. Stand as a light in your community. Shine bright. Do you see the other lights flickering in the distance? They are those living sent in neighboring communities. Lights are shining all over the world from those standing as the sent ones, dwellers of purpose, doing their part in their corners of the world. Pick up hope, O traveler. Hold on to it, for you can't even imagine how you will need it.

We All Play a Part

Where we are being sent next doesn't catch God off guard. You might start a conversation about faith while at the office with your coworker, but it's someone at back-to-school night who will get to pray with her as she tells them about her recent divorce. And she experiences the peace of God for the very first time.

His roommate watched him cling to the Word of God and wanted to know how it was making a difference in his studies, choices, and lifestyle. It was months later when the roommate gave his life to Christ.

My friend Mrs. Emy has rocked hundreds of babies in the nursery room of her church, including two of my children. She voices prayers of intercession over their lives as she pushes back and forth on her toes, lulling them to sleep and keeping them happy while their parents are in church. She's done this for so long, she's now able to see them as adults when they come back to visit.

I want to exclaim one day, when I see a former classmate at the gates of heaven, "You're here! Who told you more?" I want to know.

The end. Oh, no. Not the end. To be continued. I wait with expectation for my friends in the city to see that Jesus saves and that He loves. Their faces are right before me as I write this to you. You've got names and faces too. I pray even now for the millennial I met at the Halloween carnival, that she will step into our church family one day, that someone at her popular tech company will demonstrate God's love, and that she'll want to know where it's from. We play our part and trust in the Sending God to position others to water, sow, and reap in the very stories we bravely stepped into for a season.

To Be Continued Stories—Ongoing Stories

We are all living in "to be continued" stories. We are sowing into some and reaping the harvest in others. God has the final word. Until then, He's moving us around, making introductions, opening our eyes to the very people He has created whom we are to love.

Several people on our journey have caught back up to encourage us with these sweet words from Psalm 40: "You have multiplied, O LORD my God, your wondrous deeds and your thoughts toward us; none can compare with you! I will proclaim and tell of them, yet they are more than can be told" (v. 5).

> Guess who is teaching kids at church? Rekha the nurse. She's also bringing friends, family, and colleagues to church with her. Rekha is not living in fear of what they might think of her for asking about their faith. Her faith has great value to her.
>
> When Darren got baptized at our church, his mom and family, plus Darrell and other coworkers, filled the rows closest to the well of water. I was in view of the baptism and the people who are visuals that Darren is not alone in his position.
>
> The boys and I learned compassion from "Homeless Hannah" and have learned to pray immediately when we see brokenness on the streets. We also keep packs of crackers in my bag to meet the hunger needs of the homeless in our city. They are on our sidewalks every day. We make the choice to interact with them. When I buy a package of peanut butter crackers, I always get two, one for the house and one for the streets. When I am on King and 4th Street, I intercede for Hannah. I pray someone else is pouring into her life.

Stephanie now calls Boston home because of a family career move. I got to see Stephanie growing in her faith in San Francisco. Her baptism was such a sweet celebration as a dozen or so moms stood up throughout the auditorium during her declaration. When she left, she made sure she packed two things from her time as a dweller here: a greater desire to build community quickly and a greater desire to learn about the people around her, making friends of diverse cultures and backgrounds. I am confident she's in the business of sowing and reaping in Boston. I envision us getting to rejoice together in the heavenly city, the sowers and the reapers.

Remember two-year-old Sam praying for Josh for two years? Josh ran the soundboard in the early days of our church plant, teaching himself and a volunteer team. He continues to serve at our church. He's met his wife in the city and is a faithful friend. With their influence in this city, their story is an ongoing one.

Anna, who reached out for a granola bar and invite card, came to church with her toddler son, Zach, for some time. Her husband, Brian, enjoyed having peace and quiet around the house on Sunday mornings. One week, he decided to tag along and find out what this was all about. He kept coming and eventually wanted a Bible. He came to faith. They welcomed a daughter into the world, and she has never known life without a faith-filled community. Their son, Zach, came to faith. I can point to several women in our church who say they come because a lady named Anna invited them. This started with a granola bar and an invite card. It's why we live sent.

Do you remember our neighbor on Day Street who cracked his door open just enough to receive our welcome bag? Later on, we would call the police on suspicious activity in his driveway while he was out of town. It happened to be early on a Sunday morning, when we were up because of work while the rest of the block slept in. We crouched down low by our front window to witness a potential break-in. The police arrived and took care of the situation. He learned that we had called it in. It's what God used to open up the door.

God gives our kids the insight to see that our stories are still being written and are intertwined with others'. Asher chooses to pray for a friend at his school who has a hard time controlling his temper and getting along with others. It was a happy day when Asher shared that this friend had asked him what he would do in a certain situation. "Just be yourself," Asher said. "You can't go wrong if you give them you." The following day, this classmate of his reported that he took Asher's advice. This was huge. Asher got to see the fruit of his prayers and God at work in this friend.

One of the names on Sam's wall is a classmate who's become a friend. Four days into kindergarten, this boy's mom introduced herself to me and said that if it weren't for Sam, her son would have stayed in bed. They went through elementary school together, and his name has stayed on the wall to remind Sam to pray for his friend. After six years, this family was in a hard place and decided to take us up on one of many invitations to come to church with us. Their story isn't over yet!

Remember Cathy, who was baptized with her parents? Cathy's parents now have a sign displayed in their home in China: "Christ is the Lord of my family." It's their constant reminder of what God has done for them.

Alin moved to the States and plugged into a faith family after moving from his home in Romania, and a partnership was birthed between Epic Church in San Francisco and Impact Church in Oradea, Romania.

We do what we can with our gifts, then we let others pick up where we left off. Alan, dwelling in Ireland, told one of his

American colleagues, Mary, about the church he attends when he is in San Francisco. She was relocating there and was at a place where she needed something to cling to that was beyond herself. She gave this church a try and found family instantly. After several weeks, Mary decided to place her faith in Jesus and make her life about Him. As she shared her story at her baptism, she mentioned Alan as the one who had invited her, and the difference that made. Guys, our stories are not over yet. Neither are theirs! The kingdom of God is massive.

800,000

I listened with hundreds of others at a conference. I heard, "Are you dreaming big enough?" And the number 800,000 flashed in front of me as if on a big marquee. That's about the number of citizens in my city. That's my dream. That's God's dream. To see 800,000 people in San Francisco know the love of Jesus. How small I'd been dreaming! When 800,000 is the dream, I stay connected to a limitless God. It's beyond my reach but not His. He is not limited to my network or neighborhood. Ben and Lindsey can host dinner with other couples in their townhouse and they, too, are touching the 800,000. God can be found in chai bars and next door to the corner store. He is in rural America and along the coast. The three people I got to love today . . . well, that's 799,997 left to go.

Mother Teresa humbly served the people around her in small ways, but she delighted in knowing that God sees everything on a grander scale. As she served, she said:

> I never look at the masses as my responsibility. I look only at the individual. I can love only one person at a time. I can feed only one person at a time. Just one, one, one. You get closer to Christ by coming closer to each other. . . . So you begin . . . I begin. I picked up one person—maybe if I didn't pick up that one person I wouldn't have picked up the others. The whole work is only a drop in the ocean. But if we don't put the drop in, the ocean would be

one drop less. Same thing for you. Same thing in your family. Same thing in the church where you go. Just begin . . . one, one, one.[1]

If we leave the big stuff up to important people who have to be about the large tasks, then it's you and me who get to do the ordinary stuff like smiling, touching, crossing the street, giving a hand, listening to their stories, and giving sacrificially. May it never be said of us that in our town, on our watch, we wanted to serve but decided it was too dangerous, too messy, and too unpredictable. Start right now.

Is your life set up in such a way that unless God shows up, you've got no chance? Then your story isn't over. Remember His faithfulness. Recall what He has done for you. Reminisce about the carefree moments when you weren't overthinking His provision but were dancing in it. Go to the end of your life and ask what you want it to have been about. Start there and live it in reverse. You'll know who you touched and who touched you. You won't be thinking of grocery lists and crumbs on the floor, of weight loss plans or your grades. What will matter most is who you loved: the least of these, the enemy, the persecutor, the neighbor, the religious person, the immigrant, the wealthy, the poor.

Jesus said, "Truly, truly, I say to you, whoever believes in me will also do the works that I do; and greater works than these will he do, because I am going to the Father" (John 14:12).

DWELLER TIP

I'm learning not to run home to my roots when it gets messy in the city but to stay in the messy and see the beauty of God.

—Praise, photographer and creative

28

Global God

People are living sent all over the world in this very moment. Everyone has a story. Every culture has a past. Dwellers of purpose are trying, imperfect in their own strength but perfect in Christ. God takes our efforts and sends out ripples that go global. He is at work all over His earth.

Alin moved to the States and plugged into our faith family after moving from his home in Romania. His story wasn't over. Because of his love for his homeland and the church, two churches separated by thousands of miles became connected.

Come with me to Eastern Europe, to the western part of Romania, to a town called Oradea, and to a people recovering from communist rule that crumbled in 1989. We're standing in the local community hospital, the lowest of priorities as the people work to rebuild and trust again. This is why Florin and Nico, dwellers of Oradea, make it a point to love the least of these and do so as unto God.

"You understand me?" Florin asked me this because he thought his English was weak, but I believe he also asked to make sure I was grasping the depths of his story. Our church team was painting when Florin wanted to show me more.

He showed me their first renovation—a dilapidated room turned into a chapel. Around the corner was an area that looked like a bomb shelter to me, but not to Florin. This would one day be a clinic where doctors would teach and learn. Over there would be a prep area for doctors getting ready for surgery. That section would be a place to treat those with addictions.

How I want to see how Florin sees! He then took me down the hall to a neglected and overcrowded storage room. A black table was turned on its side—the collected dust on its surface making it perfect for drawing the story he wanted to share.

The times were communist and he was a teenager. His father was told to renounce all of his property or go to jail for eighteen months. He chose jail and still lost his property. The thinkers, pastors, doctors, professors, and teachers were all being thrown in jail, allowing the communists to brainwash and control everything.

Florin drew a building in the dust. Communists created a factory that controlled all electricity and hot water and would turn it off and on at their liking. Florin would have to stand in line for staple groceries that were being rationed out and had no access to decent food.

He drew a house and a church, then tapped on the church. Communist leaders moved into the governor's house. They didn't like looking at the Hungarian church that was across the street, so they made plans to tear it down. The Hungarians and Romanians stayed inside that church building for three weeks. The communists didn't tear it down. Unity among the believers was strong.

This was so much to take in—to realize that I was listening to a story told firsthand from communist days in the twentieth century. Florin was a passionate man with a story always on his lips. He was just getting started, for this story is of his home, the place he has loved since he was a young man, through the trials and the pain. I looked around at all the furniture and books and what-not.

He picked up a stack of books and blew the dust away. Then he tapped number after number that had been stenciled on the beds, tables, chairs, and cabinets. I wanted to know what they meant.

Florin spoke with passion. "All public property was given a number by communist leaders so that it could not be stolen. Every piece in a school, hospital, or government building had a file and was registered. For them to get rid of anything, each piece has to go before a committee to deem it trash. That's why it's all still sitting in this trash pile, forty years after the fall of communism."

My friend Lisa called it old. Florin called it trash and pointed to himself.

"I'm old, but I'm not trash. This is trash!" He told us he needed an update, like the hospital we were standing in, but didn't need to be thrown out!

It would be Pastor Florin, Pastor Adi, and their families who decided to stay and not flee Romania when communism fell and everyone else seemed to be running for the border. They were determined to love the very place that held hurt and pain and fear of the unknown. This determination would be in the daily living and daily struggles to stay and not go. To trust God with the uncertainty and not give up and leave. Learning to love again would take time.

Over time the medical staff and the patients noticed that a church in their community cared enough to put in new windows and add a fresh coat of paint to the hospital. Over the years, a Swedish company saw the repainted rooms and bought new beds for the post-surgery rooms. Before this, the staff would have to constantly move the recovering patients on and off the old beds to adjust them. Local lawyers showed up while our team was there to help propel the cleanup work forward.

The director of the hospital took notice. She saw volunteer teams come and paint freely and with such care. She started occasionally attending Florin's church. She got her husband to come to the Christmas service, and he said he had no idea this was what Christmas was all about!

Florin pointed her out to me. She had even shown up on Saturday, her day off, to help our church team paint her hospital!

And one of the doctors treated our team to lunch as her way of saying thanks.

· · · · · ·

The hospital is not the only place where love is coming to life among the hurting in Romania. Up the road and around the bend is a home for the elderly. I saw more of the glory of God in a few hours there than I have in a lifetime. Living sent invites you into the story that God is writing, and when you step into it, God introduces you to those who are both overqualified for any Nobel Prize and invisible to world leaders. Yet they have the audience of our Savior, and I am certain He is overjoyed to see His faithful leading strong, with their eyes fixed on the heavenly city.

The founder of this home saw a need among the elderly, who had been discharged from the state hospitals but had no family to care for them. When he opened the first home, he was able to take in fifty severely disabled and mentally unstable elderly people. There are now over two hundred men and women living in the ten homes this founder has purchased in order to care for the least of these. He received no financial funding from the state, but they are the very ones who brought the sick to him.

A caregiver opened up the gate to let us onto the property. Our team gasped in unison. Somehow we put one foot in front of the other as we stepped into what looked like a war zone. The elderly were dispersed among the grounds. Piles of chopped wood formed a hill in the center of the property. The earth was uneven. We looked like foreigners—and felt like it too. But we showed up to meet their greatest need for the day, stacking wood for the winter so they could keep warm and cook food. We were quietly working, our senses taking in gulps.

Under an awning, dozens of older men watched us. Florin told us that many of the elderly had been professors and teachers in their prime. I wondered what they thought of us and how we could be doing a better job. An ambulance arrived. It was a daily activity, taking someone away or bringing someone to them. The founder conducted seven to ten funerals a month. He saw it as providing dignity, for without this home they would have died all alone on the streets.

While working, I had a self-talk. The people around us were dependent upon God for their daily bread with limited care and medical access, and no family to stop by and see them. Yet God saw them. God knew they were there. God knew their names.

Say the name of Jesus over this place, Shauna. This got trapped in my head. *Say the name of Jesus over the people.* I couldn't get it out. I was moving back and forth, from woodpile to stack. Sawdust was below my feet and flying around us as we worked. No one else knew I was unbalanced in my thoughts. I wanted to say it, but it wasn't coming out of my mouth. *What was going on?* I looked at my team. We were all working hard. I uttered softly, "Jesus."

"Jesus, in Your name, I speak healing. In Your name, Jesus, move among the people here. Jesus, provide abundantly. Send more workers. Increase the strength of the caregivers. Like You speak in visions to people, speak to these beautiful people here in visions and dreams. Bring salvation here. I speak the powerful name of Jesus here. You are welcomed in this place."

I'm not sure if Florin heard my quiet words or if he just had another story to tell, but I'll take his stories any day.

He told me of a time his car broke down. He was furious at his car. He had no choice but to take it to the mechanic. The mechanic was so happy. Florin's suffering was the answer to the mechanic's prayer. "I now have work today and can feed my family," the man told him.

Florin pointed to the woodpile as we came close to finishing up for the day.

"I have to also cut and stack my own wood, but when I come and do it here, Jesus ends up warming our home miraculously," he said. I was working in the miracle in a place that was so far from home, but so close to God. "You understand me?" Florin asked. I heard him say, "Go live in obedience and God will take care of the rest."

I know of four miracles that happened up the hill and around the bend at the elderly home that day. A man showed up before we got there with lots of meat. Another man walked onto the property and said his wife had heard of this place and they were passing through today. They had bags of onions, beans, greens, and a wheelbarrow load of eggplant. Another mission team would come after us and finish stacking the wood.

We went in to wash up and get ready to leave. Four elderly men were playing chess. One spoke English. He told us that his friend beside him couldn't speak at all but copied Scripture out of the English and Romanian Bible on sticky notes and passed them out. His name was Putina, and he slipped me one of his notes.

DO NOT CONFORM TO THE Pattern OF THIS WORLD, BE TRANSFORMED BY THE RENEWING OF YOUR MIND. THEN YOU WILL BE ABLE TO TEST AND APPROVE WHAT GOD'S WILL IS—HIS GOOD, PERFECT AND PLEASING WILL. ROMANS 12:2

My friend Stefanie also received a Scripture from Putina, and said it well: "I had no idea I had brothers and sisters here!"

. . . . . .

The best inspiration this side of heaven is our brothers' and sisters' stories of miracles in the suffering. This Romanian town is just one corner of the world, yet God is using His people in corners all over the world! We are everywhere, sent ones. In a living room in Kinsale, Ireland. On a patio in London, England. In the streets of Kampala, Uganda. In the middle of the Pacific on a Coast Guard ship. In a nursery of a church in Tuscaloosa, Alabama. In the offices on the forty-second floor of a business in Taiwan.

Where are you going, short-term or long-term, that needs to hear the name of Jesus? Having a hard time with an employer?

Not understanding what is being taught in the classroom? Feeling like an outsider? Seeing injustice happen on the street or in a certain part of town? Drive through the area. Walk around the block. Speak His name. He is working miracles around the globe and around the corner.

Pray this prayer written by pastor Pete Scazzero: "Grant me the grace to follow You into the next place You have for me in this journey called life."[1]

On the world map, put dots where you have heard or are hearing of God's activity among His people, and put dots where you know believers are living sent. My prayer is that as you hear stories and meet people, your map will be covered with God's activity!

We're not alone. Where we live now or where we might move one day, dwellers of purpose—people of faith—are at work. Travel with hope as you board the plane and open the door. "You understand me?"

DWELLER TIP

Living in a new culture, new country? Visit locals' homes. It is revealing of their priorities and their interests, and you quickly learn what is culturally normal as they play the role of host so comfortably and beautifully.

—Chris and Caryn, Nairobi, Kenya

God's Activity Map

29

Heavenly City

As she arrives, no one at the gate is checking for paperwork, documents, certificates, report cards, diplomas, or proof of citizenship. It's a good thing, since she came empty-handed. It's the same for everyone who came before her, is arriving at the same time, or will come later. No goods, money, pleasures, shopping bags, or earthly stuff is being brought into eternity.

As she walks along the streets of gold, barefoot, she wonders, *Will there be classmates of mine here? Will my neighbors be here? I know most of my family is here, but what about my aunt and uncle? Will there be people in the Great Smoky Mountains who heard and believed when we did that musical the summer of 1990? What about that school mom? That lawyer at church? That postal worker?*

This believer is now standing before the very throne of God. She looks around and fidgets with her hands. Having just left a busy earth, she hasn't been in the heavenly city long enough to settle into the worship and grandeur.

She blinks, and suddenly she's surrounded. The throne room of God is full yet spacious. She's amazed at who is beside her.

She smiles to the Asian girl from her Louisiana days, who has her family with her. She sees the student from camp, who gave his life to Jesus. All around her are the people who put their faith in God on her watch, in her time, because of His love on display in her. There might not be any tears in heaven, but something incredible happens as she turns and sees high school girls, schoolteachers, sales clerks, city officials, friends of her children—people from every tribe and nation she visited. She didn't know if they would be here. Someone else must have watered where she planted, reaped what she sowed.

• • • • • •

It's a dream I've had since I was young. I first dreamed it in my daybed in the town of six traffic lights, and it's resurfaced on mission trips, at vacation Bible schools, and at camp. The picture comes to mind every time I hear songs about heaven. And while the dream undoubtedly pales in comparison to the reality, I hold on to the hope that one day my faith will be made sight and I will see those I've prayed for and those I've talked to about Jesus.

Envision what can be our eternal reality. For me, I've declared it for years, sometimes with strength and courage and at other times with little faith and an empty tank. While sitting in a Baptist church with a heavy heart, praying that my friends would believe and that my community would wake up. While in the bleachers on campus, declaring it over my future, not able to lean on my parents' faith or my friends' purpose but only able to give my all to Him. I've gone to Rajasthan, Hong Kong, Guadalajara, Vancouver, and St. Petersburg, and declared this anthem, praying for the people to know Jesus loves us and, on top of that, He saves. Alongside my church family on Sundays, I envision heaven, including those I'm singing with now and will sing with then. I look over and I see Bill—his hand extended from his soul, including all that he experienced that week in his worship. I hear Rachael's voice behind me as she declares that she believes. The people with whom we moved to start this church are singing with so much passion.

Who Will Stand beside Us As We Represent Our Corners of the World?

Jim Elliott, Nate Saint, Ed McCully, Roger Youderian, and Pete Fleming stand beside the Auca tribe in the heavenly city.[1] They moved to Ecuador as missionaries to tell the people about Jesus. The men spent months winning favor and gained their trust—just not from all of them. Auca warriors killed these men who lived sent for their sake that they may know Jesus. How did the Auca tribe get to heaven?

Jim Elliot's widow, Elisabeth, their daughter Valerie, and Nate Saint's sister, Rachel, picked up where the men had left off. People of the tribe came to trust in God all because these women didn't give in to fear of man, for their fear of God was greater. How incredible the moment when Jim encountered people from the Auca tribe arriving in the heavenly city!

"Who told you?"

"Your wife and daughter!"

And You

In the heavenly city, it's not just who we notice but who notices us. Mother Teresa had the credentials to teach us what we can take with us to our final dwelling place: "At the end of our lives, we will not be judged by how many diplomas we have received, how much money we have made or how many great things we have done. We will be judged by 'I was hungry and you gave me to eat. I was naked and you clothed me. I was homeless and you took me in.'"[2]

And you. And you. And you.

And you kept inviting me, though I kept telling you "some other time." And you gave me a ride home after all those ball games, and I heard the love you had for one another. And you went out of your way to make sure I had a place to go for the holidays. And you stood by my side at work even though you knew my past. And you saw past my color. And you saw me as a person, not a disability. And you lived right next door. And you invited me over. And you worked with my son. And you held my hand. And you spoke to me because you saw me.

Life is not intended for isolation but community. To fulfill Jesus's words in Matthew, we need one another. But that's not the issue, is it? We've got people all around us. We need unbelievers in our lives. We need to be loving, listening, praying, walking, going, looking, and serving. We need to get to the heavenly city and to the end of this life and hear someone say, "And you," and another say, "And you," and another, and another.

Our earthly position won't matter in the heavenly city, except in how we leveraged it. I see people thanking the mom who packed her son's lunch that fed the five thousand. Mary Magdalene tells Joseph of Arimathea that she's been to one of his tombs. Wise men and shepherds high five, as they were some of the first to see Jesus. Generations of Ninevites find Jonah to say thanks. Abraham says to everyone he sees, "You're a star. And you. And you. And you." He gives a deep belly laugh.

Same Address

All the longing in us for greener pastures, cleaner streets, perfect climate—it's found here in the heavenly city. Our longing for them wasn't the problem; it's an innate part of us. It just wasn't to be fulfilled on earth but in heaven. That's why we look forward. That's why we feel the tension. We're not home yet.

God built and designed the heavenly city. It's perfect. Abraham exercised faith in what he couldn't see and went where he was called to go because he believed a time would come when his faith would be made sight before his Maker in the city of God.

All these people were still living by faith when they died. They did not receive the things promised; they only saw them and welcomed them from a distance, admitting that they were foreigners and strangers on earth. People who say such things show that they are looking for a country of their own. If they had been thinking of the country they had left, they would have had opportunity to return. Instead, they were longing for a better country—a heavenly one. Therefore God is not ashamed to be called their God, for he has prepared a city for them. (Heb. 11:13–16 NIV)

While it's hard to see friends move away, let me remind you that we'll all have the same address one day. Until then, I've got people over here to tell and you've got people over there to tell, so that even more may share our eternal address. For in the heavenly city, it doesn't matter where we lived on earth. All followers of the One True God have the same address.

It will all make sense then. We'll see how every story ends. The ones you poured yourself into and the ones you did a kind deed for in His name. The sacrifices you make on earth are reaping dividends in His kingdom. The little things that no one else sees, He is paying attention to. He is networking from on high, and He is working all around the city limits that we may all be with Him in the heavenly city.

I'm not even going to say that the heavenly city could be boring, but have you ever been to a party without knowing anyone but the host? The heavenly city celebration will be all the better when you are reunited with those you touched here on earth. Sure, we'll all see Jesus, but don't you want to see your neighbors, colleagues, classmates, baristas, and teammates too? For the "least of these" in your very town to find you and thank you?

Jesus Face-to-Face

A day is coming when we will see Jesus face-to-face. We will chant His name victoriously. Everyone will bow before the Greatest King, the Greatest Servant, Emmanuel, who came to be with us. The One we spent our time on earth seeking and pointing others toward. Nothing else matters at this point but the lives we lived and the God we adore.

. . . . . .

The girl glances over to the person beside her, and he's covered in compassion stickers, like she is. They smile, knowing the pain, hurt, and tears are no more. A gentle hand touches both of their shoulders. The compassion stickers disappear.

"Welcome home," He says.

DWELLER TIP

Raising kids in the city is stellar because it's how we'll live in heaven. The exception being we'll get to run the streets of gold barefoot like rural folks!

—Liz, from North African cities to Honolulu, Hawaii

A Few More Introductions

It's been a delight to have you on this journey through our cities and towns and across the globe. I'm so thankful to the people who have met us along the way. They are so kind and brave to share their stories. It's the countless others with whom I didn't seek permission whom I want you to meet and want to thank.

Carolyn McCready saw this story unfolding in its early days and told me to keep writing.

There was an empty spot at the writers' table for this introvert, so I sat down. The Supper Club was born, and we have clung to each other ever since, sharing wisdom and shouting encouragement. Robin, Rachel, and Mandy, your tea stains are all over these pages.

Katy Hamilton let me knock on her door many times so she could enhance my proposal.

Andrea Doering was just another conference attendee, or so I thought, until I glanced down at her nametag. We talked about city living, and God breathed such a sweet communion over our friendship that weekend hidden in the California mountains. She saw the vision of this book and, by a leap of faith, brought me in. The ripples of this book are because of her yes.

I've learned in the making of this, my first book, that writing is a team effort. And I'm absolutely certain I've had the best with Jennifer Nutter, Brianne Dekker, Cheryl Van Andel, Lindsey Spoolstra, and the whole team at Revell.

We are better at living sent when we have a friend beside us, seeing better, loving deeper, and calling us to a more authentic version of ourselves. God gave me Lindsey Lee.

Lining the sidewalks, sometimes on their knees and sometimes with pom-poms in their hands, are Dad, Mom, Natalie, Katie, Matthew, the Bagwells, the Rainwaters, and the Pilgreens. Family should look like this.

It's Ben's fault, really, this crazy adventure we're on. I'm not upset. He smiles as I talk to a stranger and helps me wash the dishes after countless dinners with friends and neighbors. He wants me to use up my gifts here on earth. He even lets me borrow his sermon notes, leadership thoughts, and date day wisdoms, some of which have worked themselves into this book. And what is wrapped around this book are the 6:17 a.m. prayers from our chairs he offered up with much faith.

My kids are conversation starters and manuscript interrupters. I'm so glad. Stepping away from writing to help do homework or cook dinner or floss teeth readjusted my eyes and my heart every time. It is Elijah, Sam, Asher, and Kavita who live this Jesus principle so well. They are leaving marks of kindness and light all over this great city.

Step inside and see my faith family, standing and singing each Sunday with battle cries and songs of love for the God of the city, unified, with hands held high, believing God. Epic family, your faith fuels mine.

Jesus is the Author of my life and the Awakener of my soul. The Holy Spirit is the Author of this book. God is the Creator of these *only God* stories. What is written is by God's grace, for He is who saves, calls, and equips.

Maybe you left your heart in San Francisco when you came to visit or live. Mine is still here. I don't love her perfectly but enough that I won't stop living sent until everyone here knows the love of Jesus Christ.

This book is profoundly *us*.

Notes

Introduction Why Live Sent?

1. Jane Jacobs, *The Death and Life of Great American Cities* (New York: Random House, 1961), 238.

2. Shauna Pilgreen, *Live Sent: 31 Days in the City*, extended ed. (The Send Network: Alpharetta, GA, 2015).

3. Hannah Whitall Smith, *The Christian's Secret of a Happy Life* (Chicago: Moody, 1883), 19.

Chapter 3 Thanks, Queen Esther

1. Philip Yancey, *Prayer: Does It Make Any Difference?* (Grand Rapids, Zondervan, 2006), 210.

Chapter 4 Start to Stay

1. Maria Goff, *Love Lives Here* (Nashville: Broadman & Holman, 2017), 29–30, 8–9.

2. Kurtis Alexander, "The Great 2014 Pier 39 Sea Lion Disappearance," *SF Gate*, June 28, 2014, http://www.sfgate.com/bayarea/article/Famed-sea-lions-vanish-from-Fisherman-s-Wharf-5585563.php.

Chapter 8 Meet the Neighbors

1. Jacobs, *Death and Life of Great American Cities*, 92.

Chapter 9 Meet the Faith Family

1. Brian Zahnd's words are used by permission.

2. Norman Grubb, *Rees Howells: Intercessor* (Fort Washington, PA: CLC Publications, 1952), 279.

3. Grubb, *Rees Howells: Intercessor*, 279.

4. Tricia Neill, *From Vision to Action: Practical Steps for Church Growth* (London: Alpha International, 2013), 49.

5. C. S. Lewis, *Mere Christianity* (New York: Harper One, 1980), 64.

Chapter 10 Walking Shoes

1. Thought inspired by Dr. Aseem Malhotra and Donal O'Neill, *The Pioppi Diet: A 21-Day Lifestyle Plan* (New York: Penguin Books, 2017), 122.

Chapter 11 Seeing Eyes

1. Mark Buchanan, *The Rest of God: Restoring Your Soul by Restoring Sabbath* (Nashville: W Publishing Group, 2006), 5.
2. Buchanan, *The Rest of God*, 5.

Chapter 13 Compassion Stickers

1. Dr. Samuel Johnson, *The Rambler*, March 24, 1750.

Chapter 16 Circles

1. Tim Keller, Twitter post, @timkellernyc, February 22, 2017, https://twitter.com/timkellernyc/status/834418472415350784.

Chapter 17 Hubs

1. Jen Hatmaker, *For the Love: Fighting for Grace in a World of Impossible Standards* (Nashville: Thomas Nelson, 2015), 118–19.
2. Pilgreen, "Appendix B," *Live Sent: 31 Days in the City*, 207.

Chapter 19 Strategic Family

1. Jane Jacobs, *Dark Age Ahead* (Toronto: Vintage Canada, 2004), 34.

Chapter 20 Position Matters

1. Parker J. Palmer, "Introduction," in *Leading from Within: Poetry that Sustains the Courage to Lead*, edited by Sam M. Integrator and Megan Scribner (San Francisco: Jossey Bass, 2007), xxix–xxx.
2. Palmer, "Introduction."
3. Grubb, *Rees Howells: Intercessor*, 279.

Chapter 21 Connector

1. Fredrick Buechner, *Wishful Thinking: A Seeker's ABC* (San Francisco: Harper San Francisco, 1993), 119.

Chapter 22 Storyteller

1. Courtney Cvetko Kiser, "Dr. Maya Angelou: It All Started with a Cable Car," *San Francisco Travel*, July 6, 2016, http://www.sftravel.com/article/dr-maya-angelou-it-all-started-cable-car.
2. "History of the Cross," Mount Davidson Cross, accessed May 30, 2018, http://mountdavidsoncross.org/about.
3. Leo Widrich, "The Science of Storytelling: Why Telling a Story Is the Most Powerful Way to Activate Our Brains," *Life Hacker*, December 5, 2012, https://lifehacker.com/5965703/the-science-of-storytelling-why-telling-a-story-is-the-most-powerful-way-to-activate-our-brains.

4. Tiffanie Wen, "Inside the Podcast Brain: Why Do Audio Stories Captivate?" *The Atlantic*, April 16, 2015, https://www.theatlantic.com/entertainment/archive/2015/04/podcast-brain-why-do-audio-stories-captivate/389925/.

Chapter 23 Grace Giver

1. *Strong's Concordance*, s.v. "2603. chanan," accessed July 16, 2018, http://biblehub.com/hebrew/2603.htm.

2. Henri J. M. Nouwen, *Reaching Out: The Three Movements of the Spiritual Life* (New York: Doubleday, 1975), 52.

Chapter 24 Intercessor

1. Grubb, *Rees Howells: Intercessor*, 262.

2. Grubb, *Rees Howells: Intercessor*, 264.

3. Grubb, *Rees Howells: Intercessor*, 265–66.

4. Grubb, *Rees Howells: Intercessor*, 302.

5. Renovare Britian and Ireland, "Rees Howells Biography," *Inspirational Christians*, accessed May 31, 2018, http://www.inspirationalchristians.org/biography/rees-howells/.

6. Neill, *From Vision to Action: Practical Steps for Church Growth*, 95.

Chapter 25 Caretaker

1. Mark Batterson, *Wild Goose Chase: Reclaiming the Adventure of Pursuing God* (Colorado Springs: Multnomah, 2008), 50.

2. Buchanan, *The Rest of God*, 63.

3. Peter Kreeft, *I Burned for Your Peace: Augustine's Confessions Unpacked* (San Francisco, Ignatius Press, 2016), 14.

4. John Ortberg, "The Soul Needs a Center," *John Ortberg*, April 22, 2014, http://www.johnortberg.com/the-soul-needs-a-center/.

Chapter 26 Your Story Isn't Over

1. Jill Briscoe, "If:Gathering 2017," November 9, 2017, video, 44:42 (see 19:20), https://www.tellingthetruth.org/watch/individual-post/videos/2017/11/10/if-gathering-2017.

Chapter 27 Their Story Isn't Over Either

1. Michael Colloy, *Works of Love Are Works of Peace: Mother Teresa of Calcutta and the Missionaries of Charity* (San Francisco: Ignatius Press, 1996), 35.

Chapter 28 Global God

1. Pete Scazzero, *Emotionally Healthy Spirituality Day by Day: A 40-Day Journey with the Daily Office* (Grand Rapids: Zondervan, 2014), 80.

Chapter 29 Heavenly City

1. "Jim Elliot: Story and Legacy," Christianity.com, July 16, 2010, https://www.christianity.com/church/church-history/church-history-for-kids/jim-elliot-no-fool-11634862.html.

2. Colloy, *Works of Love Are Works of Peace*, 35.

Raised in a ministry home in rural south Georgia, **Shauna Pilgreen** now finds herself immersed daily in the reality of doing life in the global city of San Francisco. She and her husband, Ben, started Epic Church in the heart of downtown in 2010 and have been *living sent* ever since. Shauna is the mother of three boys and an adopted daughter from India.

Connect with **Shauna Pilgreen** at
www.ShaunaPilgreen.com

Praise Santos
@comeplum
comeplum.com

shauna.pilgreen@gmail.com

@ShaunaPilgreenStory   @ShaunaPilgreen   @ShaunaPilgreen